YOU'VE GOT MAIL

Copyright©2002 Spring Harvest

Jeff Lucas asserts the moral right to be identified as the author of this work.

Published by
Spring Harvest
14 Horsted Square
Uckfield
East Sussex TN22 1QG

First edition 2002

Text of pages 140–160 copyright© 2002 Crusade for World Revival

Acknowledgements
Scripture quotations taken from the HOLY BIBLE, NEW INTERNATIONAL VERSION.
Copyright ©1973, 1978, 1984 by International Bible Society.
Used by permission of Hodder and Stoughton Limited.
All rights reserved. "NIV" is a registered trade mark of International Bible Society.
UK trademark number 1448790

Quotations attributed to Mike Smith are gratefully acknowledged. They are from a
manuscript (currently unpublished) by Mike Smith, entitled "What happened next?"

Please note that the inclusion of a quotation or example in this book does not imply
endorsement by Spring Harvest.

Printed and bound in Malta.

Spring Harvest. A Registered Charity.

ISBN   1 899 78839 5

Journeying with Jesus

Jesus writes to his church

Spring Harvest 2002
Study Guide

by Jeff Lucas

SPRING HARVEST

Equipping the Church for action

Using your Study Guide

At the beginning of each section is a MENU – an overview of the material that follows. Then there's a BIBLE PASSAGE from Revelation 2 or 3 with space for you to write some notes.

Following is the MAIN COURSE – the body of the material itself. The MAIN COURSE is served up in two-page helpings, and is a resource centre. The left-hand page contains the main body of the teaching material, with relevant quotations and references in the left margin. Throughout the text the [Press to reply] boxes draw your attention to key questions raised by the teaching material. LINKS on the right-hand page point to more information that amplifies or illustrates the teaching material.

At the end of each section there are two extra items: first a series of questions and material to help you think through the practical application of the day's material to your local church; second some specially written material on marriage.

The envelope logo ✉ introduces relevant text from one of the letters to the seven churches in Revelation 2 and 3.

Virus warnings ⚠ warn of dangers and things that can go wrong for individuals or churches.

RESOURCE LINKS
references to books, web sites or organizations.

A book.link 📖 is a pointer to a book you might like to read to study a particular issue in greater depth.

A Web.link [www] provides details of a web site or page on the internet where you can find further information.

FURTHER INFORMATION LINKS
more detailed material to complement the core teaching material.

A past.link ⏱ is a historical link giving a perspective from history that illustrates the subject.

A plus.link ⊕ is more detail, perhaps a book extract or research paper that amplifies or comments on the material.

A theo.link ✝ contains more detailed theological or doctrinal material.

Introduction

Spring Harvest is 'journeying with Jesus' over a three-year period. Two years ago we began by learning from the character and person of the Lord Jesus, particularly using the perspective of John's gospel. Last year, we examined the Sermon on the Mount (Matthew 3-5) and asked how we should be applying it to our lives, churches and communities today.

Now in 2002, we look into the last book of the Bible – Revelation – to discover a vision of Jesus Christ as our Lord who is now risen, ascended and glorified. But the glorious Christ is not out of touch with his church. He took the trouble to 'send mail' to some young and struggling churches in the first century. Those letters are recorded in Revelation chapters 2 and 3 – and they are sharply relevant to us today.

Contents

Journeying with Jesus
You've got MaiL
Jesus writes to his church

NOTES

Daily menu

A living community

Christ is the one who was dead but is *alive forever* and he is looking for a church that is genuinely alive – rather than reputedly so. We will explore the text of the words to Sardis and Laodicea in the Bible Reading, examine some 'signs of life' in the Zones, and then see the vital life that Jesus enjoyed and shared compared with the dead orthodoxy of the synagogue official.

Bible passages

Zone outline

Church audit

Evening Celebration

Luke 13:10–17, the healing of the woman on the Sabbath.
Jesus shows living faith, the synagogue official shows dead faith

Jesus writes to his church

BIBLE PASSAGES

REVELATION

3:1–6   Sardis

1"To the angel of the church in Sardis write:

These are the words of him who holds the seven spirits of God and the seven stars. I know your deeds; you have a reputation of being alive, but you are dead. 2Wake up! Strengthen what remains and is about to die, for I have not found your deeds complete in the sight of my God. 3Remember, therefore, what you have received and heard; obey it, and repent. But if you do not wake up, I will come like a thief, and you will not know at what time I will come to you.

4Yet you have a few people in Sardis who have not soiled their clothes. They will walk with me, dressed in white, for they are worthy. 5He who overcomes will, like them, be dressed in white. I will never blot out his name from the book of life, but will acknowledge his name before my Father and his angels. 6He who has an ear, let him hear what the Spirit says to the churches."

3:14–22   Laodicea

14"To the angel of the church in Laodicea write:

These are the words of the Amen, the faithful and true witness, the ruler of God's creation. 15I know your deeds, that you are neither cold nor hot. I wish you were either one or the other! 16So, because you are lukewarm—neither hot nor cold—I am about to spit you out of my mouth. 17You say, 'I am rich; I have acquired wealth and do not need a thing.' But you do not realise that you are wretched, pitiful, poor, blind and naked. 18I counsel you to buy from me gold refined in the fire, so that you can become rich; and white clothes to wear, so that you can cover your shameful nakedness; and salve to put on your eyes, so that you can see.

19Those whom I love I rebuke and discipline. So be earnest, and repent. 20Here I am! I stand at the door and knock. If anyone hears my voice and opens the door, I will come in and eat with him, and he with me.

21To him who overcomes, I will give the right to sit with me on my throne, just as I overcame and sat down with my Father on his throne. 22He who has an ear, let him hear what the Spirit says to the churches."

NOTES

_____
_____
_____
_____
_____
_____
_____
_____
_____
_____
_____
_____
_____
_____
_____
_____
_____
_____
_____
_____
_____
_____
_____
_____
_____
_____
_____
_____
_____
_____
_____
_____
_____
_____
_____
_____
_____
_____
_____
_____
_____
_____
_____

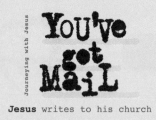

Journeying with Jesus

You've got Mail

Jesus writes to his church

Aims of this session:

■ Give a broad overview of the context of the letters to the seven churches, introducing the fact that all of them were under pressure – and that faith is normally worked out under pressurized rather than tranquil circumstances.

■ Demonstrate that Jesus speaks to a people under pressure who felt somewhat deserted – and that Revelation is designed to realign and encourage struggling believers, not as an apocalyptic puzzle book.

■ Show that Christ calls for a living faith today – past accomplishments and progress are just that, so we must continually ask ourselves whether we are really alive.

■ Explain some of the symptoms of Christian sleeping sickness – and the steps outlined by Christ to find our way back to life again.

THE CHURCH – A LIVING COMMUNITY

Back to the future

Imagine it for a few moments. You are a follower of Jesus, and a member of a local church – but in your city, there is but one Christian church that meets and worships together. Your nearest neighbouring church is over forty miles away. No easy transport system links you to them, but the Roman roads would have allowed you to make the journey by horse in under a day. You do have a common bond with those other churches, in that you all share a special relationship with a leader who has influenced both you and them – but he himself has been threatened, tortured, and has now been deported because he is a Christian.

There are no opportunities to celebrate together, Spring Harvest style, with other believers. No Christian resources are available. No Christian books to encourage you. No New Testament to give you hope.

It's been a rough, turbulent few years. Earthquakes have shaken the land you live in. Massive political uprisings have seen unprecedented bloodshed. Some of the social foundations of your culture have been dug up. Everyone is tense about the future – whatever next?

You and your church are under threat. Your neighbours are suspicious of you, and you live under the daily possibility that they will report you to the authorities for being an atheist, as they term it. Your city is infested with occultism and paganism. Everywhere you look are signs of the great power base Satan has established in your locality. You've turned to other religious groups to try to find some shelter with them, but they are now reporting you to the authorities.

National political leaders are feeling insecure, and are starting to talk about loyalty to them and to the state being the only acceptable worship. You wonder … will you bow the knee to them one day? Some of your brothers and sisters in Christ have turned away from faith because of the pressure.

This satellite photo shows how the highway linking the seven churches of Revelation wound between the mountains of western Turkey, following the river valleys.

7 churches

… I heard behind me a loud voice like a trumpet, which said, "Write on a scroll what you see, and send it to the seven churches; to Ephesus, Smyrna, Pergamum, Thyatira, Sardis, Philadelphia and Laodicea."

Rev 1:11

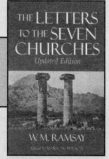

The Letters to the 7 Churches, W.M. Ramsay/ M.W. Wilson, Hendrickson

The Letters to the Seven Churches of Asia in their Local Setting, Colin J. Hemer, Eerdmans

"The Christians of Asia certainly had the feeling of being under fire. They were under threat from the Jews from whom they had once derived some protection. They faced the possibility of an uncomfortable ride with the pagan authorities. The temptation to keep a low profile and avoid mention of Christ in any conversation must have been very great. If only they kept quiet, they might be left undisturbed."

– Stephen Travis

With all of this chaos, it must seem to you like the end of the world is coming. And that has been your hope – that Jesus would come back, and bring his kingdom order into the madness and the chaos. But then, that's the worst of it. Because heaven is silent. And then **suddenly you hear the news…**

You've got mail.

Seven under pressure

The situation you've just been imagining was quite close to the experience of the seven churches of Asia, described in Revelation 1–3. As the first century drew to a close it was a time of turbulence for those early believers – in some limited cases even a time of persecution. Nero had begun his persecution of the Christians twenty-five years earlier – mainly in Rome – but now the Emperor Domitian was in charge, and the reverberations of his antagonism were beginning to be felt in Asia. The apostle John was in exile on the Isle of Patmos.

The seven churches were:

- Scattered over a wide 200-square-mile area in western Turkey
- Surrounded by major pagan and occult influences in every strata of their culture
- Mutually linked in a relationship with the apostle John. Other churches existed (like Colossae) that didn't share the same apostolic link with John
- Relatively small groups of people in significant cities, without any church buildings
- People who had experienced the cataclysmic events of earthquakes, military coups in Rome, the Jewish revolt of AD66 and the resulting destruction of the Temple in Jerusalem in AD70
- Under heavy pressure from continuous tension between Christians and Jews, who regarded them as atheists
- Increasingly under threat from the totalitarian rumblings of Emperor Domitian, a dangerous man with a major inferiority complex who liked to be addressed with the worshipful greeting *dominus et deus* (lord and god)
- Struggling with an ever-increasing tax burden levied by the imperial authorities
- Facing the challenge of some Christians giving up their faith
- Facing the challenges of heretical teaching and false prophecy in the churches – some of which were encouraging immorality
- Hopeful for the return of Jesus – yet nothing seemed to be happening.

JOHN ON PATMOS

Patmos, a barren, rocky island, is just 8 miles long and 5 miles wide. It sits about 40 miles off the Asian mainland, about 65 miles from Ephesus. John was not necessarily there as a prisoner, but if not, he was probably banished there by the proconsul of Asia – rather like the orders imposed by Communist authorities on dissidents during the cold war years.

It seems likely that John had been forcibly separated from the seven churches, with whom he had a special relationship, due to ongoing tensions with Jewish and pagan groups. As he writes, he does so with an awareness that the clouds of persecution are quickly gathering for his beloved fellow believers. He writes to strengthen them in this time of increasing pressure. He was not a missionary to Patmos, but an exiled servant of Christ (Rev 1:1) who was paying a high price for his faith. This is the person to whom Christ comes with his revelation.

PAGAN INFESTATION

Once a Christian had been exposed as a potential troublemaker, he would be expected to demonstrate his loyalty by offering worship to Rome and its emperor. Apart from the possibility of falling foul of the governing authorities in this way, there was the constant pressure of the pagan atmosphere that surrounded every Christian. As they walked the streets they were always conscious of the temples and statues of pagan gods, the obscene graffiti, which covered many a wall, and the symbols of the old fertility cults that retained a prominent place in popular religion. If we today are exposed to the potentially harmful influence of the media, the absence of television and advertising hoardings in first-century Asia did not leave people free from such onslaughts on their minds. The gods themselves were not simply remote mythical figures. Although Christians had given up worshipping these gods, they knew the continuing power of all that they represented. We, too, may dismiss as childish the stories which were told about the gods, but we are just as likely as an ancient Greek to be seduced by the ruinous power of sex, or alcohol, or money or a thousand other 'idols'.

– Adapted from You've Got Mail, *Stephen Travis, Spring Harvest*

CHRISTIAN/JEWISH TENSIONS

Judaism enjoyed a special privilege as a recognised religion that Jews were allowed to practise wherever they lived.

But then the situation changed – and the catalyst was money and taxes. After the fall of the Temple in AD70, the Romans decided to demand the temple tax paid by all Jews for the upkeep of the Roman temple of Jupiter. This created tensions in the Jewish communities, which viewed payment of this tax as a sign they had accepted Rome's full authority over them. But through paying this tax Jews could continue practising their religion undisturbed by emperor worship. And so the Christians began to see a clear attachment to Judaism as an attractive, viable option – which the Jews resented. Christians now had a loophole to avoid bowing the knee to Rome, at least overtly – if they attached themselves to the synagogue. Those who came from a Jewish background could obviously do this easily – and others could claim the Jewish roots of their Christian faith. The Roman authorities did not at first distinguish Christians from Jews.

There was already tension between Jews and Christians because Christians widely believed that the fall of the Temple was a sign of God's wrath and judgment upon the Jews for their crucifixion of Christ. Not only this, but it appears that Christianity was winning to its ranks a significant number of God-fearing gentiles who had previously associated themselves with the synagogues.

Now the Jews, stung by the Christian's view of judgment upon them, and resentful anyway about the growth of this new Christian movement, could inform the authorities that the local Christians were not Jews at all. The Christians were left in a situation of intolerable pressure. If they tried to remain under the cover of Judaism by offering to pay the tax to Jupiter, Jews could protest that they were not genuine Jews. If they did not pay, that only proved they were not Jews and laid them open to suspicion of being a dangerous new cult. Around AD90 the curse of the Minim was introduced into the 18 benedictions as a way of detecting Christians in the synagogues.

"Individual Jews may have informed against individual Christians, or the synagogues may have provided on occasion lists of bona fide members of their congregations. The authorities, primarily concerned with tax avoidance, may thus have had forced on their attention a powerful movement which appeared to defy the emperor under the guise of a Judaism which the official Jews repudiated. A systematic inquisition would naturally follow."

– *Colin Hemer*

"Pliny's letter to Trajan about the Christians refers to some who had abandoned their faith ... around AD92 ... possibly under social pressures."

– *Colin Hemer*

Revelation, Tyndale NTC, Leon Morris

"The gospel had been preached throughout Asia ... some had believed and become Christians ... they had been taught that Jesus of Nazareth was the Christ, the Son of God. Having died he rose triumphant now to die no more. He went back to heaven, but in due course would return ... and set up God's perfect kingdom. It was an inspiring faith and the little group of Christians embraced it with fervour. They looked and longed for the promised consummation when God's will would be perfectly done throughout the whole earth. And nothing happened."

– *Leon Morris*

virus ⚠warning 🕷 **THE HERESY THAT CHRISTIANITY IS EASY**
Pressure is more normal than ease for New Testament Christians. Jesus speaks to a people in the midst of stressful circumstances, not to those who have managed somehow to escape them.

Mind the gap

John writes to address the needs of these pressurized churches.

Revelation was written for a church stuck in the gap between promise and fulfilment. It is full of pastoral encouragement for a people feeling abandoned and fearful. There is much to encourage us too.

They've got mail, but is it for us too?

Nineteen-hundred years later, we seem a million miles from that little network of churches. Surely we would scribble 'return to sender' on this message from Jesus if it arrived in our mailbox.

We are…
- ☒ Sophisticated, awash with resources
- ☒ Those who know some little opposition, but nothing like the persecution the Seven faced
- ☒ Living in relatively stable period of social history, at least in our immediate part of the world
- ☒ Distant from totalitarian demands in our permissive, postmodern culture of relativism.

And yet…
- ☒ There is an eternal relevance in the words of Jesus about what he wants his church to be
- ☒ Apparently the words spoken individually to each church were to be shared with all seven – each message is tailor made, yet somewhat universal in its application
- ☒ We too find ourselves at every turn bumping into materialistic, pagan influences that threaten to misshape our thinking and behaviour
- ☒ Our 'strength' can be the greatest source of deception
- ☒ We know what it is to be living in the gap – there are many Christians who long for revival, yet see little sign of its dawning; who believe in divine healing, yet struggle with sickness; who work to impact their communities with the gospel, but see no obvious fruit

A LIVING COMMUNITY

MIND THE GAP

The church continued to be a tiny group, doubtless adding a few members from time to time, but not becoming, and not looking like becoming, a mighty force to take over the Roman Empire. The empire still continued on its wicked way. Oppression and wrong abounded. Evil men prospered ... and because they would not conform, the tiny band of Christians found themselves the objects of suspicion and sometimes outright persecution. A few of them were killed; some were put in jail.... What had become of the message that had induced them to become Christians in the first place? Where was the promise of Christ's coming? Had they been mistaken in coming to Christ in the first place? Was it all a delusion? Was real power in the hands of the emperor and his associates?

To a church perplexed by such problems Revelation was written. We must not think of it as a kind of intellectual puzzle (spot the meaning of this symbol!) sent to a relaxed church with time on its hands and an inclination for solving mysteries. It was sent to a little, persecuted, frustrated church, one that did not know what to make of the situation in which it found itself. John writes to meet the need of that church.

IT'S FOR YOU

Just as the letters of Paul convey the word of God to us as well as them, to London, New York and Cairo as well as to Corinth and Thessalonica, so Christ's letters through John to the first century Christian communities of Asia have a permanent value and a universal message.

The devil's tactics do not change. As we look around the world today, the same pressures are harassing different churches. In some areas of the world open hostility to the gospel. In others, intellectual combat with an insidious ideology or a materialistic philosophy. Elsewhere the struggle is in the moral field ... the book of Revelation is a call to us to endure tribulation, to hold fast to the truth, to resist the blandishments of the devil and obey the commandments of God.

– John Stott

"John presents us with a vision of how Christ wants the church to be. This is the kind of church we need to be ... whether in the first century, or in the twenty first century ... the letters meant for them are meant for us also."
– Stephen Travis

book.link

What Christ thinks of the Church, John Stott, Candle Books, 1990

"Even though the words of Christ refer initially to the first century churches located in particular places, by the Spirit's continual relevance they transcend that time limitation and speak to all the churches in every generation."
– Frank E. Gaebelein

"The book of Revelation has not been appreciated in recent years as it should. It has become strangely overlaid by the oddest assortment of views and interpretations! It has become the playground of the cults. Ordinary Christians have left it unread, turned off by the mathematical labyrinths in which some of its readers appear to have become enmeshed."
– Richard Bewes

"The book of Revelation, is, I fear, a very neglected book. This is unfortunate because its theology of power is of the utmost importance to an age as preoccupied with the problems of power as ours."
– Leon Morris

18

We've got mail – and it's to be found in the book of Revelation

People either ignore Revelation, with its strange language and bizarre symbols, or become obsessed with it.

Revelation is one of the most misunderstood books of the Bible. It's the plaything of cultists, and it's often been turned into a mystery book, an apocalyptic puzzle rather than a call to genuine discipleship in the face of great pressure. Revelation is about Jesus, and his power and might – it is "The revelation of Jesus Christ" (Rev 1:1).

virus ⚠warning 🕷 **PREDICTABILITY**
To each of the seven, Jesus says; "He who has an ear to hear..." Are we open? Ready to hear the unexpected? Do we acknowledge that the church belongs to Christ – and he can say what he likes and do what he wants with her? Are we counting ourselves in – or feeling smug about our church?

We've got mail – and it's about Jesus

The churches under pressure didn't need a puzzle book or a conundrum to occupy their attention – they needed a fresh vision of Jesus.

They were living in a culture where many saw Caesar as lord – Emperor Domitian had been celebrated by the poet Statius as being like "the morning star". But in Revelation John lets his readers know that there is only one who is worthy of such an illustrious comparison – Jesus, the Christ.

He is revealed as the one who is:
- ✉ Not distant – but walking among the candlesticks (Rev 2:1)
- ✉ Not ignorant – but knowing (Rev 2:2)
- ✉ Not silent – but speaking (Rev 1:12)
- ✉ Not subject to forces of chaos – but Lord of history, working to a plan (Rev 5:1–2)
- ✉ Not impotent – but Lord over death and hell (Rev 1:18)

virus ⚠warning 🕷 **THE CLICHÉ BUG**
People under pressure don't need encouraging rhetoric – we need an authentic, greater vision of who Jesus is.

Patmos – the island of the revelation – just below a cave where John may have received his vision.

THE EVIL EMPEROR DOMITIAN – REAL PERSECUTION OR ANCIENT SPIN?

It is commonly thought that Revelation was written during a Roman persecution of the Christians in the latter years of Domitian's reign. This is due to historians and scholars putting a great deal of store by the words of Eusebius, who states that many people fell victim to Domitian's appalling cruelty and were executed, banished and fined in the later part of his reign. But Eusebius wrote many decades after Domitian's reign. The internal evidence of Revelation hardly supports the view that the Apocalypse was addressed to a situation dominated by martyrdom. The only martyr mentioned by name is the Antipas of Rev 2:13, and it is far from certain how this person died.

The idea that Domitian was an evil despot comes from various ancient sources. Suetonius (c.70–c.160) for instance, says that from an early age Domitian 'exercised all the tyranny of his high position so lawlessly, that it was even then apparent what sort of a man he was going to be'. Tacitus (c.55–c.117) mentions his unbridled passions (Hist 4.68); Pliny describes the imperial household as the place where 'that fearful monster built his defences with untold terrors, where lurking in his den he licked up the blood of his murdered relatives or emerged to plot the massacre and destruction of his most distinguished subjects' (Pan 48.3). It was widely discussed that he allegedly carried on an incestuous affair with his niece Julia.

Pliny (c.61–c.113) complains about the number of statues that Domitian erected in his own honour and his practise of being addressed as *dominus et deus noster* 'Our Lord and God'.

But there are some scholars (ie. L. Thompson, *The Book of Revelation, Apocalypse and Empire*) who refuse to brand Domitian so negatively, arguing that Domitian's successor, Trajan, needed to cast himself as a new style libertarian, and a hero of a new age – and for that to happen, negative spin was placed on his predecessor. One historian dismisses the so-called incestuous affair as "normal affection between and uncle and niece." The total silence about a Domitianic persecution in Christian sources before Eusebius (265–340) is significant.

Jesus writes to his church

7 churches

I turned round to see the voice that was speaking to me. And when I turned I saw seven golden lampstands, and among the lampstands was someone "like a son of man", dressed in a robe reaching down to his feet and with a golden sash around his chest. His head and hair were white like wool, as white as snow, and his eyes were like blazing fire. His feet were like bronze glowing in a furnace, and his voice was like the sound of rushing waters. In his right hand he held seven stars, and out of his mouth came a sharp double-edged sword. His face was like the sun shining in all its brilliance.

When I saw him, I fell at his feet as though dead. Then he placed his right hand on me and said: "Do not be afraid. I am the First and the Last. I am the Living One; I was dead, and behold I am alive for ever and ever! And I hold the keys of death and Hades."

Rev 1:12–18

"Christians down the years have fondly assumed that churches are automatically on the side of God, and he is on their side. The letters of Revelation show this to be a dangerous delusion."

– Stephen Travis

We've got mail – with a few surprises

Over the course of the next few days, we'll discover that Jesus had some shocking and surprising things to say to his churches. Will we open our ears and listen to him?

virus ⚠warning 🕷 **THE 'THEY' BUG**

We've got mail. It's about 'us' – not 'them'. We can develop a tendency to step outside the church when we criticize it – 'they' have problems – forgetting that we are part of 'they'. But the local church is a sum of its parts – we are part of its strengths, and its weaknesses. We own and identify the challenges humbly.

And so, let's open our mail …

We will not look at the seven in the order of the biblical text: with only four days in Zones to explore the material, some grouping together of the material has been necessary.

❖   The Church as LIVING community
Sardis and Laodicea

❖   The Church as LOVING community
Ephesus

❖   The Church as LOYAL community
Pergamum and Thyatira

❖   The Church as LONG SUFFERING community
Smyrna and Philadelphia

WE'VE GOT MAIL – AND IT CONTAINS A FEW SURPRISES

▶ We tend to think that "our church is right, and okay." After all, it is church, isn't it? We can easily write off those who disagree with our positive diagnosis as being rebellious, damaging individuals that are a threat to unity: the enemy. But churches seem to have a tendency towards self-deception; sometimes we need to listen to the voices that sound disturbing and subversive.

▶ We often think of Jesus as 'nice' and 'safe'. Surely he would only speak words of comfort and pastoral concern to a people who were going through pressure – wouldn't he? But even when his people are going through trial, Jesus is still willing to speak shocking words to wake them up.

▶ We tend to think that 'good' Christians have got sound doctrine and full diaries. Christian service and biblical orthodoxy are both vital, but if a church becomes a group of stern, hard working people who forget to love God and God's world, then Jesus is not pleased.

▶ We can become obsessed with being 'relevant' to such an extent that we are more concerned about a cool, seeker-sensitive image than we are about what Jesus thinks about his church. And that should be priority Number One.

▶ Surely it's a disaster when a church building is closed down and turned into a furniture store – isn't it? But what if Jesus decided to close the church? Christ is not committed to just sustaining what is, just because we call it church. He threatens to close a loveless church down for good, removing its candlestick.

▶ Church can be a battleground, and it's just because we're all human – isn't it? Blaming the devil for everything is unbalanced. But behind the scenes, there is an invisible battle raging around and in our churches. It's a battle in which Christ and Satan are involved.

HE WHO HAS AN EAR ...

We all have two sets of ears. One set, of course is our natural ears. Even before we are born, most of us are able to hear sound; although sometimes, as our physical faculties deteriorate with age, we may become deaf. The other set of ears is invisible, and contrary to the way it happens in life, we are born deaf. The fact is, our second set of ears do not pick up sounds and will not work unless the Holy Spirit enables us to hear in a new way. It is with this second set of ears, spiritual ears, that we hear God speaking to us. It is wonderful when we hear with both sets of ears. Every minister knows what it is like to preach and find that people only hear with their physical ears. So all they think about during the sermon are the preacher's mannerisms, oratory, eloquence and his style. Sadly, that is all some ever take in. It was to the second set of ears – our spiritual ears – Jesus referred in the Parable of the Sower when he said; "He who has ears to hear, let him hear" (Mark 4:9). Then in Rev 3:20 Jesus again spoke of our spiritual hearing when he said; "Here I am! I stand at the door and knock. If anyone hears my voice and opens the door, I will come in and eat with him, and he with me."

– R.T. Kendall

7 churches

Write, therefore, what you have seen, what is now and what will take place later. The mystery of the seven stars that you saw in my right hand and of the seven golden lampstands is this: The seven stars are the angels of the seven churches, and the seven lampstands are the seven churches.

Rev 1:19,20

Sardis

To the angel of the church in Sardis write: These are the words of him who holds the seven spirits of God and the seven stars.

Rev 3:1

Laodicea

To the angel of the church in Laodicea write: These are the words of the Amen, the faithful and true witness, the ruler of God's creation.

Rev 3:14

SARDIS AND LAODICEA

The churches of Sardis and Laodicea both had tendencies towards spiritual sleep and death.

Christ is revealed to them as the awesome victor of LIFE. "The seven spirits of God" (Rev 3:1) is usually interpreted as referring to the Holy Spirit and his wide range of LIFE-giving ministries. He is thus the living, active, energetic God – and without him we drift into spiritual sleep and death. The Spirit of Christ, the Holy Spirit (Rom 8:9) is the "Spirit of life" (Rom 8:2). The Nicene Creed declares the Holy Spirit to be both "the Lord" and "the giver of life."

- The churches at Sardis and Laodicea had seen better days – just like the cities in which they made their home.

Sardis was a city with an illustrious past – but a less-than-glorious present. An earthquake had devastated the city around 80 years earlier. Rebuilt with Roman money, it never quite recovered its glory days. Its greatness lived on in the folklore and memories of its citizens. Ancient writers often used Sardis as a byword for the pride that comes before a fall – and of arrogance and over-confidence.

Laodicea was a banking and judicial centre and like Sardis, had a thriving textile industry; in their case they were famous for clothing made from local black wool. Laodicea also had a prominent medical school that specialized in ophthalmology.

The churches in these two cities came from an uncertain background. Nothing is known about the history of the Sardis church – and, although there is some speculation, no-one knows exactly how the Laodicean congregation was formed.

Want the bad news – or the bad news?

In his words to the other churches, Christ normally begins by speaking words of encouragement and affirmation – the good news – before moving on to the bad news about their failings. Each of the seven letters has a consistent literary structure.

But with the believers at Sardis and Laodicea, there was no good news preface – they were sound asleep, and needed the jolt of a

UNLOVING CRITICISM

We will see that Christ has some very strong words of rebuke for the sleeping and dying church. But we MUST remember that his words are spoken from a heart of love and not from a heart of negativity or the excessively critical attitude that develops when we allow ourselves to be cynical about church. Even the Laodicean church – the least worthy of the seven – was assured by Christ that he loves her – hence his discipline. The Lord disciplines the ones he loves (Prov 3:12). The church certainly has plenty of weaknesses – but she is still the bride of Christ, the object of his love. Remember that we as individuals have plenty of imperfections too!

SARDIS

Sited on a major crossroads, it was a busy trade centre; it had been the capital city in the old kingdom of Lydia. Here King Croesus, reputedly the richest man in the world in his day, reigned in splendour. Sardis had been a gold rush city; gold had been found in the river that ran through its heart, the Pactolus; Sardis had also developed itself as a major fashion and textile centre. But it had fallen on hard times; even though it had thought itself invincible, it had been captured by two great generals. Pride in its own strength had been the cause of this city's downfall.

THE CHURCHES OF SARDIS AND LAODICEA

Paul probably never visited the churches of the Lycus valley, but he did write a letter to the Laodicean congregation at the same time as his letter to the Colossians (Col 4:16). Some think (on slim evidence) that the letter that we know as Ephesians was first sent to the Laodiceans. Epaphras (mentioned in Col 1:7, 2:1, 4:12–16) may have been the founder of the Laodicean church. Paul also asks for greetings to be passed on to the Laodicean church via his Colossian letter (Col 4:15) and mentions "Nympha and the church in her house" in the same greeting.

You've got Mail

Journeying with Jesus

Jesus writes to his church

"Sardis was one of the great cities of primitive history: in the Greek view it was long the greatest of all cities."

– *Sir William M. Ramsey*

"We need to see the beauty of the bride – not just her veil trailing in the mud."

– *Pete Philips*

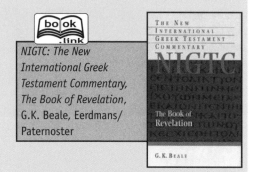

NIGTC: The New International Greek Testament Commentary, The Book of Revelation, G.K. Beale, Eerdmans/ Paternoster

New International Biblical Commentary, Revelation, Robert W. Wall, Paternoster

 **Sardis**

I know your deeds; you have a reputation of being alive, but you are dead. Wake up!

Rev 3:1,2

 **Laodicea**

I know your deeds, that you are neither cold nor hot. I wish that you were either one or the other! So, because you are lukewarm – neither hot nor cold – I am about to spit you out of my mouth.

Rev 3:15,16

firm yet loving wake-up call. Sardis heard the blunt indictment: they were dead. And Laodicea suffered a similar alarm call: they were lukewarm – and their actions made Jesus sick. Thus we see a key point:

Churches – and Christians – seem to have a natural tendency towards being sleepy and dead

Two of the seven churches are in grave danger, three are neither very good nor very bad, and two are in good shape. The trend is towards decline.

The sleeping sickness of the Christians at Sardis and Laodicea was evident because they were:

- ⌧ Complacent and not watchful (Rev 3:2)
- ⌧ Starting projects with enthusiasm, but then leaving them unfinished (Rev 3:2)
- ⌧ Morally compromised (Rev 3:4)
- ⌧ Completely ineffective (Rev 3:15–16)
- ⌧ Self-deceived (Rev 3:17)

Press to reply

† Are we alert and alive?

† Do we look back on earlier enthusiasm for Jesus with a sense of having 'become wiser' – but realise that with our 'wisdom', apathy has also arrived?

† How engaged are we with people and activities outside our church – or is most of our life spent in church activities?

† Change is a sign of life: the dead are static. So how well do we and our churches do with change?

Staying alive 1:

Check your pulse today – and don't believe your own publicity

Don't lean on your past, particularly if you have enjoyed a good reputation: churches with 'good' reputations are sometimes particularly sedated…

FORM LETTER

The letters are more in the nature of messages than letters. Each message to an individual church was apparently also intended for the other six churches. Each message generally follows a common literary plan consisting of seven parts:

1. The addressee is first given.
2. Then the speaker is mentioned. This identification is preceded in each case with the significant declaration "These are the words of him" – a declaration strongly reminiscent of the Old Testament formula for introducing the words of God to the congregation of Israel.
3. Next, the knowledge of the speaker is given. His is a divine knowledge. He knows intimately the works of the churches and the reality of their loyalty to him, despite outward appearances. Each congregation's total life is measured against the standard of Christ's life and the works they have embraced.
4. Following his assessment of the churches' accomplishments, the speaker pronounces his verdict on their condition in such words as "You have forsaken your first love" (2:4) or "You are dead" (3:1).
5. To correct or alert each congregation, Jesus issues a penetrating command. These commands further expose the exact nature of the self-deception involved.
6. Each letter contains the general exhortation "He who has an ear, let him hear...".
7. Finally, each letter contains a victor's promise of reward.

– Frank E. Gaebelein, Expositors Bible Commentary,

WATCHFULNESS

Several times during his public ministry, Jesus told his followers to watch. The word was often on his lips. His disciples must watch and pray; they must be dressed ready for service with their lamps burning and be like men who are waiting and watching for their master to return from the wedding banquet (Luke 12:35–37). Some scholars have suggested that the command to be watchful was particularly appropriate to Sardis because this almost impregnable city had twice fallen to surprise attacks.

– John Stott

THE SLEEPING CHURCH

There are some telling symptoms in Laodicea and Sardis that we might find in the sleeping church today. The church that:

▶ Lives in the past
▶ Leans on the laziness of extra-biblical rules and regulations
▶ Has stopped believing that there are new paths to take
▶ Has become an internalized club for like-minded people, or a costless country club
▶ Is more concerned with portraying a positive image than expressing the character of Jesus
▶ Is busy with the club activities rather than service to local community
▶ Believes in evangelism but never practices it
▶ Hides behind an excessive, controlling commitment to 'decency and order' rather than allowing the disturbance of the Holy Spirit
▶ Degenerates into a weekly session of ecstatic worship where everyone turns up just to get an emotional high
▶ Tells enthusiastic people they will 'get over it'
▶ Sees church as haven from change rather than agent of change
▶ Confuses frantic activity with spiritual activity
▶ Points to its programme as evidence of life
▶ Begins projects, but never completes them

– is likely to be asleep!

c The Church stop Changing, then the church stops the being the church

"It's not hard to imagine the church in the West sprawled like a beached whale, eventually dying because it has been cut off from society. All that needs to happen is for congregations to persist in what they do now."

– Michael Moynagh

Changing world, changing church, Michael Moynah, Monarch Books 2001

www.christian-research.org.uk

"Through the failure to watch in the city of Sardis ... the acropolis had been successfully scaled in 549BC by a Median soldier, and in 218BC by a Cretan."

– International Standard Bible Encyclopedia

Writing about the people of Sardis, Herodotus (fifth century BC) described them as, "the tender footed Lydians, who can only play on the cithara, strike the guitar, and sell by retail."

REPUTATION IS A DANGEROUS THING.

virus ⚠warning 🕷 Don't rest on your laurels, a reputation easily can become outworn and false as it is:

- ⊠ Normally based on popular perception, and therefore inaccurate
- ⊠ Sometimes created by association – because we know the right people, or because the minister of our church is well known and highly respected
- ⊠ Usually related to the past, and therefore not current
- ⊠ Something that has the power to blind us to the reality of our condition – we "believe our own publicity".

Just as Sardis was living in the powerful deception of past reputation, so the people of God there had fallen under reputation's spell.

The church at Laodicea also had a good reputation and 'knew the right people' – we've already noted that Paul took care to greet them via the Christians in Colossae (p23).

When church depend on the Reputation of the Past

Both churches seemed 'alive', but in fact they were a perfect model of inoffensive, ineffective Christianity.

then the church loosing their meaning

Your 'good' reputation is highly dangerous – to you. Reputation can cause us to view ourselves through the clouded eyesight of someone else's perception of us.

Press to reply

† Do you have a 'reputation' in your church? Is it true?

† Is your church a 'reputed' church? In what ways does it live up to its reputation, and in what ways does it fall short?

† How can we live in the tension of having a "good reputation with outsiders" (1 Tim 3:7) without falling into some of the traps that reputation brings?

A LIVING COMMUNITY

Looking toward the necropolis of Sardis across the valley from the acropolis. In the valley is the Temple of Artemis.

MORE ABOUT SARDIS

Death was a special preoccupation of the Sardisians, as witnessed by the impressive necropolis seven miles from the city. There are hundreds of burial mounds visible some seven miles from Sardis.

"The church in Sardis was a community of the living dead."

– Robert W. Wall

"Content with mediocrity, lacking both the enthusiasm to entertain a heresy and the depth of conviction which provokes intolerance, (the church at Sardis) was too innocuous to be worth persecuting."

– Caird

"Sardis was a city of peace, not the peace won through battle, but the peace of the man whose dreams are dead and whose mind is asleep, the peace of lethargy and evasion."

– William Barclay

"Like the city of Sardis itself, the church there had belied its early promise. Its religious history, like its civil, belonged to the past."

– R.H. Charles

"The church in Sardis: its reputation as a progressive church had evidently spread far and wide ... it was known by the other six churches in the province for its vitality. 'What a live church you have in Sardis!' visitors would exclaim with admiration ... and so no doubt it appeared. Its congregation was probably quite large for those days ... while its programme doubtless had many excellent projects. It had no shortage of money, talent or human resources. There was every indication of life and vigour ... but this socially distinguished congregation was a spiritual graveyard ... it had a name for virility, but had no right to its name."

– John Stott

"The particular expression of the lethargy of the church at Sardis was in not witnessing to their faith before the unbelieving culture."

– G.K Beale

Letters to the Seven Churches, William
Barclay, Abingdon, 1957

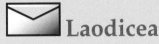Laodicea

You say, 'I am rich; I have acquired
wealth and do not need a thing.'
But you do not realise that you are
wretched, pitiful, poor, blind and
naked. I counsel you to buy from
me gold refined in the fire, so you
can become rich; and white clothes
to wear, so you can cover your
shameful nakedness; and salve to
put on your eyes, so you can see.

Rev 3:17,18

Staying alive 2:
Continually declare dependency

Churches sometimes think they <u>have everything</u>, when in fact they
<u>have nothing.</u>

Independence is the sense that we don't need anyone's help – not
even God's. It can creep into our life and the life of our church like
a stealthy raider.

The city of **Sardis** knew all about rude awakenings. The acropolis
of Sardis rises like a gigantic watchtower, its summit surrounded by
precipices. The people of the city were so convinced of their own
safety, they didn't even bother to post watches in time of war – until
Cyrus' men scaled the cliff face in the darkness one night in 546BC.

Laodicea had long been a wealthy banking centre. When an earthquake destroyed much of the city in AD60, the Laodiceans rebuilt it
from their own resources, declining the usual financial help from
Rome. Wealthy citizens endowed particular building programmes.
One financed a new stadium for gladiatorial contests. Another paid
for the heating of covered walkways and piped oil for massaging
at the public baths. They were well off, and pleased with their
achievements. They were proud of their independence – and now
the church there was adopting the same independent philosophy.

Perhaps the thought of a church that whispers 'we are rich … we
don't need a thing' is shocking. But an independent attitude is
expressed in many subtle ways.

We are not called to be independently accomplished apart from
Christ. We are called to live 'abiding' lives in him, so that we produce
good fruit (John 15:4).

DEPENDENCY

The Laodiceans' smugness about their wealth has a remarkably modern ring. Increasing prosperity has a numbing effect on Christians as on anyone else. We come to take it for granted that our standard of living will continue to rise. We adjust our expenditure to take account of our pay increases. The whole clutter of materialism so easily blunts our spiritual awareness. We don't have to pray for our daily bread because we know it's waiting for us at a friendly supermarket. Gradually and unnoticed, the thought steals upon us that our everyday lives can continue without much attention to God. We can save him for the difficult times, when he'll be there to help us out. We have lost the simplicity of the disciple whose eyes are sharply focused on the love and the demands of God because there is no other source of security to cloud her vision. And what is true for individual Christians is true for churches also. They can come to rely more on the wealth of their traditions, the stability of their income and the efficiency of their systems than on the living God. Even their success in winning people to faith can become a means of congratulating themselves on being superior to other churches. Once, maybe, they used to say, 'Lord, we long for you to make yourself known to us and to our neighbours, and we depend on you because without you we can do nothing.' Now they say, 'How rich I am! I have everything I want.'

– Stephen Travis

SIGNS OF THE INDEPENDENT CHURCH

- ▶ The feeling of being invincible – why wouldn't God bless us?
- ▶ Spirituality becomes perfunctory and tokenistic
- ▶ Hunger for human accolades and applause
- ▶ Entrepreneurs are listened to more than prophets
- ▶ We have all the answers – a feeling of spiritual superiority over other Christians
- ▶ Worship becomes mechanical and lifeless
- ▶ Church always sees itself in the driving seat – even in serving others. It is the church that meets needs, and doesn't view itself as having many needs that others could help them with
- ▶ Indifference to other expressions of church in the town or the city, accompanied by the spoken (or unspoken) notion that 'we really are the best church in the area anyway.'

Journeying with Jesus

You've got Mail

Jesus writes to his church

Press to reply

† Do we tend to think of faith as a characteristic only of new Christians?

† If God was not involved in your church, what difference would it make?

† Some churches seem have designed mechanisms to keep God at a distance. Can you think of examples of this for your own church?

† When was the last time you made a decision that required risk and dependency on God?

† Jesus says: "Apart from me you can do nothing" (John 15:5). Do our actions suggest that we don't believe him?

> "The words of Christ to the Laodiceans describe vividly the respectable, nominal, rather sentimental, skin deep religiosity which is so widespread among us today. Our Christianity is flabby and anaemic. We appear to have taken a warm bath of religion."
>
> – *John Stott*

> "A body moving without proper connection to the head is not accomplishing something worthwhile or noble. It is experiencing a seizure, or a spasm. Spasmodic churches don't bring a smile to the face of Christ, but cause a spasm in his throat."
>
> – *Jeff Lucas*

Staying alive 3:
Don't just be busy – be fruitful

Churches busy doing nothing – ineffective – make Christ sick.

The city of Laodicea faced particular challenges because of its lack of a hot or cold water supply. They had to suffer lukewarm water – and Jesus calls them away from lukewarm faith.

virus ⚠warning **LUKEWARM**
The words of Jesus about his desire that we be hot or cold but not lukewarm have been mistakenly understood to refer to spiritual passion. But this is not the case.

✉ In this analogy, cold is good, because cold water is good for drinking! Coldness of heart could not be commended by Christ

✉ Christ makes clear it is the deeds or works of the Laodiceans he knows to be insipid. Lukewarm water is good for nothing (just as salt that loses its saltiness "is no longer good for anything, except to be thrown out and trampled by men" Matt 5:13), and their efforts were as useful to Christ and to the community as the tepid water that was the bane of daily life at Laodicea.

30

Water pipes at Laodicea encrusted with the mineral deposits that made the water unpalatable.

WATER SUPPLIES

The city of Laodicea faced particular challenges because of its lack of a hot or cold water supply. The nearby towns of Hierapolis, six miles to the north, boasted some famous hot springs that were excellent for bathing and medicinal purposes – and the city of Colossae, ten miles to the east, had an ample supply of cold, pure spring water that was ideal for drinking.

But Laodicea faced the daily frustration of having neither – they had to pump water in via aqueduct from the hot mineral springs of Denizli, which was five miles away. The result? Lukewarm water that was tainted by calcium carbonate deposits – water fit for neither bathing nor drinking – just insipid enough to turn the stomach.

According to a survey we conducted among 1600 active Christians in German-speaking Europe, 80 per cent could not identify their gifts. This appears to me to be one of the primary reasons why the 'priesthood of all believers' has, for the most part, never been achieved in the lands of the Reformation."

– Christian A. Schwarz

"There is a message here for those who belong to what is sometimes termed 'a dead church' and who are tempted to leave it and go elsewhere. Of course we do have to leave a church that denies the fundamentals of the faith, for then it is apostate and no longer a church. But what about a church that is orthodox but dead? Christ's will in this case is for the living remnant to strengthen what remains – perhaps by coming together and waiting upon God. A dynamic minority of awakened and responsible Christians is able by prayers love and witness both to preserve a dying church from extinction and to fan its flame into a fire."

– John Stott

WWW
http//web link

Willow Creek Community Church
www.willowcreek.org

"There are no prizes among you for good character, for what good character do you have? But if you competed for the first prize in vice, you would all win at once. ... I would willingly have visited your city without an invitation, if I had any hopes of bringing your city into harmony with morality, with nature, with law or with God."

– Apollonius, a pagan philosopher who also sent mail to the city of Sardis

Some believe it was the absence of a clear, compassionate gospel witness that made the efforts of the Laodicean church so sickening to Christ, who is the "faithful and true witness" (Rev 3:14). Gospel clarity is the issue on which the other seven churches are applauded or critiqued.

Press to reply

† Is your church involved in projects that don't really seem to achieve anything?

† How much effort, energy and finance is directed from the church towards mission, at home and overseas, versus money spent on the internal activities of the church?

virus ⚠warning **LEADERSHIP DEPENDENCE**
When we think about the effectiveness of our church and its outreach, it's tempting to think that our leaders should be sorting these things out. This is a great deception. Our leaders are not ordained by God to the work of the ministry, but rather to *equip us* for the work of the ministry (Eph 4:11,12).

The discovery and use of spiritual gifts is the only way to live out the Reformation watchword of the 'priesthood of all believers.'

How can this be achieved when many Christians do not even recognise their God-given gifting and calling?

virus ⚠warning **DEAD BODIES**
Dead bodies don't move – but dead churches do. Activity is not necessarily a sign of life and health.

At times we must conclude that the only way we can make a healthy contribution to the life and growth of the kingdom is to move church.

Staying alive 4:

Don't be squeezed into a mould

Churches that don't challenge their culture end up shaped by it.

A LIVING COMMUNITY

GOSPEL

The unbelievers of the city (Laodicea) were receiving neither spiritual healing nor life because the church was not actively fulfilling its role of witnessing to the gospel of Christ. Two reasons suggest that the issue of witness was the specific concern:

This is the issue for which all of the other churches were applauded or condemned and it would be unusual that the Laodicean situation would be different from the others; also, Christ introduces himself as the 'faithful and true witness', and since all of the self-descriptions of the other letters are uniquely suited and related to the situations of the particular churches, the same is likely the case here. If the Laodicean Christians will not own up to their identity with Christ, he will not acknowledge them at the judgment but will 'spew them out.'

– G.K. Beale

It is our task as Christians to use our gifts to serve non-Christians with whom we have a personal relationship, to see to it that they hear the gospel, and to encourage contact with the local church. The key to church growth is for the local congregation to focus its evangelistic efforts on the questions and needs of non-Christians. This 'need-oriented' approach is different from 'manipulative programs' where pressure on non-Christians must compensate for the lack of need-orientation. It is particularly interesting to note that Christians in both growing and declining churches have exactly the same number of contacts with non-Christians (an average of 8.5 contacts). Challenging Christians to build new friendships with non-Christians is most certainly not a growth principle. The point is rather to use already existing relationships as contacts for evangelism. In each of the churches we surveyed – including those that lamented having little or no contact with 'the world' – the number of contacts outside the church was already large enough so that there was no need to emphasize developing new relationships with the unchurched.

– Christian Schwarz

STUCK IN A DEAD CHURCH

Is it right to leave a church? The faithful in Sardis must have asked themselves, as we would, "How long can we stay in this dead set-up? We seem to be unable to influence the others. Should we not withdraw from them and start a new church, meeting in one of our houses?" The option of leaving their church and joining another one down the road or even in another part of town was not, of course, open to them (as is it is to many of us), since there was no other church down the road or even in another part of town. But they could in principle have washed their hands of the rest of the church and made a fresh start in a different meeting place.

But they did not. It is significant that, despite all the problems in the seven churches, there is no suggestion in Revelation that faithful Christians should withdraw from corrupt congregations and form a new church somewhere else. Instead there is the repeated emphasis that Christ holds the churches in his hand, that he calls his people to repentance and holds out the promise of restoration. In our very different circumstances, we should perhaps not rule out the possibility of moving from a church for the sake of our own – or our

children's – spiritual health, or because our church is having a negative impact in the neighbourhood, or indeed because we have gifts to offer to another church that are already present in abundance in our present church. But we should never make such a move without careful thought and prayer. Such mobility is a luxury which is not really open to Christians like those at Sardis for whom the possibility of oppression lies not far round the corner. Certainly the weight of New Testament evidence is on the side of staying where you are and drawing on God's strength to be faithful there. A survivor's guide to such a situation would include the following advice:

- Ensure that those who share your vision for a lively church keep the vision alive through informal contacts for prayer and encouragement.
- But do not become a clique separated from the rest of the church – you will not win them over unless you stick with them!
- Keep your own Christian life healthy through the stimulus of links with Christians elsewhere, for example in ecumenical groups, and through teaching received at conferences or from books or tapes.

- Communicate your vision gently but clearly with as many in the church as you can. Don't assume that everyone is against you. There are always some who lack vitality not because they are hostile to spiritual values but because they are confused through inadequate teaching.
- If you are one of the church's leaders, try to get other leaders to agree on some plans for teaching and action designed to develop full-blooded discipleship.
- If you are not a leader, prayerfully consider how the church's leaders may be helped to take responsibility for change. Tell them perhaps, that there is a desire for a Bible study and prayer group and ask them to help you start it.
- Learn from John's Revelation that there is risk and pain in playing a prophetic role but learn also that Christ has power to change people and he hasn't given up on your church.
- If in the end you believe you must leave your church, do it in a positive very. Explain to the leaders your reasons, and find a new church where your contribution can benefit others.

– Adapted from You've Got Mail*, Stephen Travis*

> "Like a chameleon, the church at Sardis simply melted into its surroundings and became indistinguishable from them. It had become outstandingly successful at the art of camouflage."
>
> – Stephen Travis

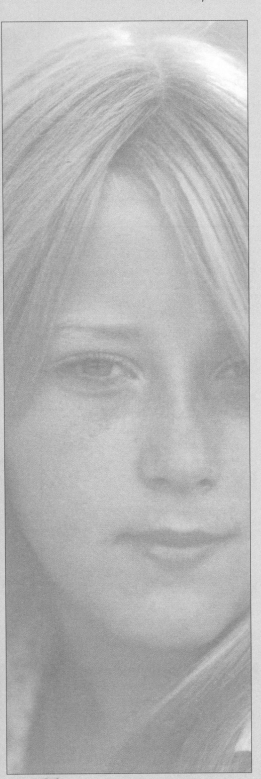

The churches of Sardis and Laodicea became very similar to the culture of their cities in their pride, independence and in their eroded view of the uniqueness of Christ. This is of special interest to us in our postmodern culture of relativism and pluralism.

The church at Laodicea seems to have been infused by the same false teaching as had developed in Colossae, which regarded Jesus as one of several intermediaries between God and human beings – hence Jesus is introduced as the Amen – the last word – of God's revelation.

- We must beware the tendency to view certainty of any kind as suspicious. While we must always speak and live with compassion as well as clarity, we should not view all dogmatism with contempt
- This means that in our desire for the church to be culturally relevant, we avoid cultural conformity
- We should beware the evangelical liberalism that refuses to pass on the news that Christ is the only way, or that is strongly committed to social action without ever being willing to "give the reason for the hope that you have" (1 Pet 3:15)
- We guard against negative elements of our culture becoming rooted in our church
- We avoid the trap of being distinctive in a superficial manner, which will prevent us from confronting the real idols of culture.

Staying alive 5:
The past doesn't determine the future

You and your church don't have to be in the future what you've been in the past. You can get a life again.

virus ⚠ warning **NO CHANGE**
The notion that you and your church cannot change is wrong.

Christ has the keys to death and hell – yet the keys to change and a brighter future are in the hands of the churches as they make choices.

- **Memory and obedience**

Reflect on the foundations of your faith – the choices that you have made about how you will live your life. Reflection like this can help us to renew our vows of allegiance to Christ.

SQUEEZED INTO A MOULD

The trouble with the church at Laodicea is that it had taken on the character of the city in which it was placed. God's people have been squeezed into the mould of the surrounding society. John's words here skilfully play on three things of which the city was proud ... yet in Christ's view the church in this city is poor.

Their second claim to fame was as a centre of medical excellence. Laodicea boasted a medical school. There was a strong tradition of ophthalmology in this area of Phrygia and ancient medical writers speak about the healing properties of 'Phrygian stone'. This was apparently a powder made from various metallic salts, including the zinc compounds that are still used in eye ointments today. Galen, the second-century medical authority who came from Pergamum, wrote: "You will strengthen the eyes by using the dry powder made of Phrygian stone, applying the mixture to the eyelids without touching the surface of the eye inside. For this is what women do every day, when they make their eyes glamourous."

We may guess from such information and from what John writes in Revelation that Laodicea marketed, extensively and profitably, an ointment developed locally. Its exact composition was no doubt kept secret from its commercial rivals. But the church in this city is 'blind'. Claiming to cure the blindness of others, it is blind to its own spiritual blindness.

Thirdly, the city was well-known for its woollen products. Numerous garments were called 'Laodicean', as we might speak of an Aran sweater or a Cashmere jumper. And Laodicea had one special advantage over its rivals. It was famous for a breed of black sheep, which Strabo (64BC–AD19) describes as follows: "The country around Laodicea produces sheep remarkable not only for the softness of their wool, which they surpass even that of Miletus, but also for its raven-black colour. And they get a splendid revenue from it."

Apparently Laodicea dispensed with the costs of dyeing for the luxury market by promoting a fashion in black glossy fabrics made from the natural fleeces of an animal developed by its own breeders. You can almost see the advertising slogan on packages of garments arriving in Rome: 'Raven-black, the Style for the Nineties'. But in this city of fine clothes, the church is 'naked'. In proud and affluent Laodicea, the church is as self-satisfied as its pagan neighbours. Thinking it has everything, it is in reality 'wretched, pitiful, poor, blind and naked'. All the banks, all the pharmacies, all the looms in the city cannot provide for its needs.

– You've Got Mail, *Stephen Travis, Spring Harvest*

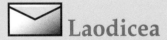 ## Sardis

Yet you have a few people in Sardis who have not soiled their clothes. They will walk with me, dressed in white, for they are worthy. He who overcomes will, like them, be dressed in white. I will never blot out his name from the book of life, but will acknowledge his name before my Father and his angels. He who has an ear, let him hear what the Spirit says to the churches.

Rev 3:4–6

Laodicea

Those whom I love I rebuke and discipline. So be earnest, and repent. Here I am! I stand at the door and knock. If anyone hears my voice and opens the door, I will come in and eat with him, and he with me. To him who overcomes, I will give the right to sit with me on my throne, just as I overcame and sat down with my Father on his throne. He who has an ear, let him hear what the Spirit says to the churches.

Rev 3:19–22

36

Note that:

Reflection must lead to ongoing obedience, not just a momentary response. The word 'obey' in the Greek is in the present continuous tense – 'keep obeying'.

The phrase 'be earnest and repent' implies urgency. Reflection should not lead to casual or partial re-commitment. We hasten to Christ for life now.

Take responsibility:

Take responsibility for your future – open the door to Christ, our friend and dining companion. The 'eating' refers to the main meal of the day.

Prioritise:

Establish what is important if we are to be in his good books. The church under pressure may find itself – as the seven did – deleted from the roll of membership in the local synagogue. It was the removal of that entry in the local book that could signal pressure from the Roman authorities, but they were comforted that their names would be eternally listed in the book of life (Rev 3:5). Our stand for Christ may mean that our names are removed from the listing of the popular, the acclaimed and the admired. But what is more important – to be in the good books of today, or tomorrow?

One day the books will be opened, and the dead will be judged by what is written in them; everyone whose name is not found written in the book of life will be 'thrown into the lake of fire' (Rev 20:15). It's a solemn fact that we can have a reputation for being alive (like the church of Sardis) and still have no entry in God's book of the living. Our name can be on a church register without being on God's register. Jesus told his disciples to rejoice that their names 'are written in heaven' (Luke 10:20; cf Heb 12:23).

Christ's gracious promise to the Christian overcomers in Sardis is that he will not blot out their names from the book of life. The Greek sentence has a double negative for emphasis, as if Jesus meant: 'I will never by any means blot out his name'. Indeed, far from removing the overcomer's name from the register of heaven, Christ promises to confess it before his Father and his angels.

There was also encouragement for some faithful believers in Sardis, the overcoming few who had "not soiled their clothes" (Rev 3:4).

REMEMBER AND OBEY

The Sardisians must remember what they have "received and heard." What they 'received' was the apostolic tradition of the gospel; what they 'heard' probably were the teachings of the apostles and prophets who brought the gospel to them. The Sardisians were not holding to the word of Christ. For them repentance was the only way out of certain and final death. So they were to repent by restoring the gospel and the apostolic doctrine to its authority over their lives, This would mean they would once more start obeying (*tereo*, 'keep' or 'watch') the truth of Christ's word. Today's church needs to hear this challenge to take the word of Christ seriously. Unless the church at Sardis repents, Christ says that he will come to them in judgment 'as a thief' – ie, by surprise – just as Sardis had been attacked and defeated by Cyrus long before. 'As a thief' should probably not be taken as referring to the Second Coming but to Christ's coming against them (opposing them) in judgment (cf. his threat to the church in Ephesus – Rev 2:5).

HIS GOOD BOOKS

Greek cities had registers with the names of the all citizens listed. It was considered a disgrace to have your name removed due to some crime. John Stott writes: "Scripture tells us that God has a book. Of course it is only a symbol; but behind the symbol is a serious truth. God keeps, as it were, a register in heaven, in which the names of his people are enrolled. It is called 'the book [God] has written', and 'the book of life', since the names of the spiritually dead are not found in it. It is also a 'scroll of remembrance', containing the names of those who 'feared the Lord and honoured his name'. Sometimes it is just 'the book', but more 'the book of life' or 'the Lamb's book of life' (Exod 32:32,33; Psa 69:28; Mal 3:16; Dan 12:1; Phil 4:3; Rev 20:15, 13:8, 21:27).

 ## Sardis

Strengthen what remains and is about to die, for I have not found your deeds complete in the sight of my God. Remember, therefore, what you have received and heard; obey it, and repent. But if you do not wake up, I will come like a thief, and you will not know at what time I will come to you.

Rev 3:2,3

"Certainly the city once prosperous and complacent is now a miserable waste. 'Nothing can exceed the desolation and melancholy appearance of the site of Laodicea,' says a twentieth-century traveller. Archbishop Trench vividly portrays the scene: all has perished now. He who removed the candlestick of Ephesus has rejected Laodicea out of his mouth. The fragments of aqueducts and theatres spread over a vast extent of country tell of the former magnificence of this city but of this once famous church nothing survives."

– John Stott

The promise to the overcoming few that they would wear white clothes would mean a lot to the Sardis faithful, living as they did in a city famous for the shame of defeat – Romans always wore a pure white toga at a victory celebration. Also, in pagan religions it was forbidden to approach the gods in garments that were soiled or stained.

RSVP

How did these churches respond to their mail?

Laodicea
changed for a while...

Sagaris, who was to die as a martyr, became church leader at Laodicea. This certainly speaks of a passionate, living love for Christ. But there were also arguments (for example, about the dating of Easter). When Sagaris died, Melito of Smyrna, an eminent and learned man, was asked to help the Laodiceans.

But gradually Hierapolis became the leading church in the region. As Mike Smith remarks, "the torch was passed on." Today, the old city is in ruins, and nothing remains of the church.

Sardis

changed for a while

The church must have taken some notice of John's message, for we find that it remained alive in the second century, and produced the remarkable leader Melito. He was a man with prophetic gifts, and was the first Christian we know of to make a pilgrimage to the Holy Land. His writings include a notable sermon on the Passover, and a petition to Emperor Marcus Aurelius arguing there was no good reason for the state to prosecute people simply because they were Christians. But within a few years, we hear nothing more of the congregation there. Melito is their greatest legacy.

The piers of one of the massive bridges that brought the famous Roman highway Via Egnatia into the city of Laodicea

The remains of a synagogue in Sardis dating from the time the early church.

MAIL FOR YOUR CHURCH

Designed for those in local church leadership, here are some questions to help you think through the implications of today's material for your congregation.

What is Church?

A vital question – Where does church happen? Who is it for?

These issues are best explored by asking lots of questions about what we do, who we are, what we want to be, and where we are heading.

The Purpose of Church

What is the purpose of church? The answer shapes how we see the church to be asleep. This has been covered already, but what does it mean? Is the church to be …

- a presence in the community?
- a place of friendships?
- a place where the truth is proclaimed?
- a place of constancy in a changing world?
- a place with people who have vision?

- a place that offers answers?
- a place where the good news is shared?
- a safe place?
- a place on the move that never stands still?
- a place where you can find or meet with God?

Select your top five in order of priority, and discuss what signs would show such a church had become sleepy.

Vital Signs

What are the real signs of life? What are your church's vital signs? Brainstorm the many vital signs present in the church? Are they the …

- type of worship?
- extent of work in the community?
- amount of resources/facilities available?
- number of weekly meetings?
- structured teaching programme?

- quality of relationships?
- openness to change?
- large diverse staff team?
- activities for all ages?
- well-kept building?

What reputation does your church have? – among both those in the church and those outside.

GETTING THERE

These questions are taken from *Getting There*, a new Spring Harvest book by Ruth Dearnley. It is a book full of questions, to be used by anyone and in any church that's open to fresh challenge and serious thinking about the future.

Some questions are general. Others apply to specific situations and challenges. Some you have asked yourself. Others are asking things in a different way.

Ruth writes; "Questions are crucial to our growing together. We need to ask them and listen to each other's answers – not to force a decision but to learn what it is that joins us, what we misunderstand and why we choose to go in a particular direction."

Getting There is on sale at Spring Harvest 2002. It is a practical book to be dipped into or worked through over a period of time. It is for all those involved in the leadership and management of the church. It is essential for anyone who wants to ask the questions that inform the way ahead.

Take it home and give it to those who have not been at Spring Harvest so that a church can talk together. You don't have to have attended the event for it to make sense. It stands on its own with a brief overview of the daily themes. Then it launches into many questions.

Take home a copy of this exciting new publication from Spring Harvest 2002.

Handling Change

▶ How does your church calculate risk – financial or other? Has it a blind plan or an informed one, an adventurous one or a safe and meticulous one?

▶ What steps you are taking have an element of risk, and how is it being approached?

▶ Is the approach working?

▶ Is a change in approach needed? Is there confusion? Is there distortion of facts?

▶ How is the consultation process moving change forward?

▶ Is it an open or closed procedure?

▶ What are the benefits of both?

▶ Who is coping with the fallout?

▶ What will completion of this change look like?

▶ How will it be marked?

Be Fruitful

▶ What is your church good at?

▶ How do you judge fruit? (*eg souls saved or people helped or increasing numbers or more giving!*)

▶ What activities bear fruit?

▶ Is there a critical level of fruitfulness to measure if something happening in your church is viable or not?

MARRIAGE ZONE

Questions to apply today's material to marriage

1. Churches can hide behind their reputations – and so can people in their marriages. "We never thought that it would happen to them" is an oft-repeated statement describing the marriage breakdown of those who were reputed to have strong marriages. But how can we open our struggles in marriage up to others without violating the security of the marriage bond? Do you occasionally do a "stock taking" of your marriage?

2. Dependency. Are our marriages alive spiritually? Is Christ's strength and grace a key part of our marriages? How can we seek to rely upon him more?

3. Busyness and fruitfulness. Do we make time for the nurture of our marriages? What are some of the key components of relational building?

4. Cultural conformity. Do we measure our expectations of our marriage according to scripture – or cultural norms?

5. The past and the future. Have we got hope for our marriages – or have we settled down, lowered our expectations and perhaps have committed ourselves to mere survival?

NOTES

Daily Menu

A loving community

Christ calls for love as a primary hallmark of his church – doctrinal purity is vital but not enough; truth without love is barren. We shall see the unity of loving God, loving one another, and loving the lost. Jesus' love towards children and the rich man demonstrate his care and love for others.

Evening Celebration

Luke 18:15–30, Jesus, children and the rich man.
Jesus shows the authentic love of God.

BIBLE PASSAGE

REVELATION

2:1–7   Ephesus

¹"To the angel of the church in Ephesus write:

These are the words of him who holds the seven stars in his right hand and walks among the seven golden lampstands: ²I know your deeds, your hard work and your perseverance. I know that you cannot tolerate wicked men, that you have tested those who claim to be apostles but are not, and have found them false. ³You have persevered and have endured hardships for my name, and have not grown weary.

⁴Yet I hold this against you: You have forsaken your first love. ⁵Remember the height from which you have fallen! Repent and do the things you did at first. If you do not repent, I will come to you and remove your lampstand from its place. ⁶But you have this in your favour: You hate the practices of the Nicolaitans, which I also hate.

⁷He who has an ear, let him hear what the Spirit says to the churches. To him who overcomes, I will give the right to eat from the tree of life, which is in the paradise of God."

NOTES

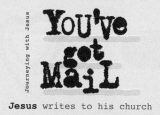

Journeying with Jesus

You've got MaiL

Jesus writes to his church

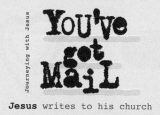

Aims of this session:

■ Demonstrate that hard work and doctrinal purity in the church are important but that love is a major priority.

■ Show that loving God is the foundation for kingdom relationships, which are far deeper than 'Christianised friendships'.

■ Show that love is practical – and is just what our communities are calling out for.

■ Challenge us with the fact that love cannot remained cloistered or isolated, but must be extended to the world that God loves.

■ Help us see that loving the world will cause us to embrace change, spend money and know our communities.

THE CHURCH – A LOVING COMMUNITY

Life in the big city

Ephesus. Sounds rural, quiet, and rurally ancient. Think again. Think about the crowded streets of London, or the cosmopolitan avenues of New York or San Francisco. Ephesus was a bustling, thriving city, loaded with people, humming with noise, the gateway to Asia.

Although Pergamum was the official capital city of the province of Asia, Ephesus was by far its greatest city. All roads, literally, led to Ephesus.

The city boasted fabulous architecture, impressive roadways, a disproportionately large population, and the most important harbour in the province. Ephesus was:

- The fourth largest city in the world, after Antioch, Alexandria and Rome itself
- A 'free' city. In the Roman Empire certain cities were free – self-governing, and exempted from having Roman troops garrisoned there. They had that honour conferred upon them because of services to the empire
- Host to the famous annual games, which attracted huge crowds of visitors from all over the province
- Graced with a 70-foot-wide road lined with pillars that led down to the harbour
- Known as 'the supreme metropolis of Asia' where the Asian governor lived
- Jammed with a population around 250,000
- Known as 'the market place of Asia Minor'
- Crowded, with homes built closely together, creating an atmosphere of noise, with the lack of privacy that intense housing brings
- Able to boast about its amazing sports facilities
- Home to a 25,000-seat theatre and the architecturally stunning Temple of Diana, one of the seven wonders of the world
- Home to another temple built to honour Emperor Domitian, with a statue of the emperor four times life size, (a giant forearm survives and can be seen in a museum) depicting the emperor as

EPHESUS – ANCIENT SPAGHETTI JUNCTION

In the time of John, Ephesus was the greatest harbour in Asia. All the roads of the Cayster Valley – the Cayster was the river on which it stood – converged upon it. But the roads came from further afield than that. It was at Ephesus that the road from far-off Euphrates and Mesopotamia reached the Mediterranean, having come by way of Colossae and Laodicea. It was at Ephesus that the road from Galatia reached the sea, having come by way of Sardis. And from the south came the road from the rich Maeander Valley. Strabo (64BC–AD19), the ancient geographer, called Ephesus "The Market of Asia". Ephesus was the gateway of Asia. One of its distinctions, laid down by statute, was that when the Roman proconsul came to take up office as governor of Asia, he must disembark at Ephesus and enter his province there. For all the travellers and the trade, from the Cayster and the Maeander Valleys, from Galatia, from the Euphrates and from Mesopotamia, Ephesus was the highway to Rome. In later times, when the Christians were brought from Asia to be flung to the lions in the arena in Rome, Ignatius (c.35–c.110) called Ephesus 'the Highway of the Martyrs'. Its position made Ephesus the wealthiest and the greatest city in all Asia.

– Adapted from The Revelation of John, *William Barclay, DSB*

TEMPLE OF DIANA/ARTEMIS

The temple was the largest building in the entire Greek world, the first to be built entirely of marble. Thirty-six of its 127 pillars, each sixty feet high, were overlaid entirely with gold – and the temple was undergoing major extension work when John wrote the book of Revelation. The temple was four hundred and twenty-five feet long by two hundred and twenty feet wide. Ancient temples consisted mostly of colonnades with only the centre portion roofed over. The centre portion of the Temple of Artemis was roofed over with cypress wood. The image of Artemis was one of the most sacred images in the ancient world. It was by no means beautiful but a squat, black, many-breasted figure; so ancient that none knew its origin. We have only to read Acts 19 to see how precious Artemis and her temple were to Ephesus. Ephesus also had other famous temples to the godhead of the Roman emperors Claudius and Nero, and in later days was to add temples to Hadrian and Severus. In Ephesus pagan religion was at its strongest.

 Ephesus

To the angel of the church in Ephesus write:

Rev 2:1

"Ephesus – the Lumen Asiae [Light of Asia]."

– *Roman writer*

"Ephesus... the Vanity Fair of the ancient world."

– *William Barclay*

 book .link

The Daily Study Bible, The Revelation of John, William Barclay, St. Andrew Press

"Ephesus was a crossroads of civilization."

– *Frank E. Gaebelein*

"The inhabitants of the city [of Ephesus] are fit only to be drowned. I can never laugh or smile, because I live among such terrible uncleanness."

– *Heraclitus, c.500BC*

Zeus, ruler of all the gods

- ✉ A city with a strong academic pedigree; an example is the Library of Celsus, the ruins of which still stand and have been carefully restored
- ✉ A city with a religious economy. Silversmiths made an excellent living from the worship of Diana – see Acts 19:23–41
- ✉ Home to thousands of priests and priestesses, many of whom were 'sacred' prostitutes
- ✉ Centre of a thriving banking system, which helped its sense of affluence
- ✉ An asylum for fleeing criminals, which helped contribute to the crime and morality problems in the city

virus ⚠warning 🕷 **NOT RELEVANT**
Sometimes we are tempted to think that the people of the New Testament would have known nothing of our pressures and stresses. The fact is, their situation is more similar to our own than we might think.

Big city church

The church at Ephesus was probably founded jointly by Aquila and Priscilla and was strengthened by extensive ministry from Paul (Acts 18:18–19, 19:1–10) who stayed longer in Ephesus than in any other city, having found an 'open door' there (1 Cor 16:8–9).

Paul tried to visit the church in Ephesus on his second missionary journey, but was 'kept by the Holy Spirit from preaching the word in the province of Asia' (Acts 16:6). On his return journey Paul visited briefly, saw the strategic importance of the city and the church, and settled there for two and a half years. He hit against the main economic and spiritual power base of Ephesus – the silversmiths who profited hugely from Diana worship (Acts 19).

Timothy was placed in charge of the church there when Paul left the city, thus Timothy was called its first bishop (1 Tim 1:3). The tender farewell speech from Paul to the Ephesian elders (when they met together at Miletus) reveals the closeness of friendship between Paul and the believers at Ephesus (Acts 20:17–38). According to tradition, John the apostle took over from Timothy towards the end of the first century. Legend has it that John brought Mary the mother of Jesus to Ephesus and that she was buried there.

SACRED PROSTITUTES

Sacred prostitutes gave legitimacy to immorality by adding a religious veneer.

The practise of sacred prostitution:
- was a flourishing industry
- was an integral part of city life in Ephesus
- combined immorality and pagan worship

Jesus commends the church at Ephesus for its perseverance and refusal to get weary or worn down (Rev 2:2,3). This is a huge encouragement for us when we feel bombarded by worldly standards of morality and choice.

PAUL IN EPHESUS

When Paul arrived in Ephesus, he found some people (twelve men; Acts 19:1–7) who had a vague idea about Jesus, but no idea about the Holy Spirit. Having given them a full knowledge of the Christian experience, Paul went to the synagogue and started outreach work among his Jewish compatriots. Soon, as was normal, he had to leave, and so he continued his preaching in a hired hall (Acts 19:9). A few manuscripts add that Paul used Tyrannus' hall from the 'fifth to the tenth hour' (11am–4pm).

It is noticeable that miraculous healings often occur when the gospel is faced by great superstition and pagan power. This happened in Ephesus to a marked degree (Acts 19:11–12). Paul's victory over the Jewish exorcists also impressed many in Ephesus, with surprising results. Those who had been involved with occult practices came and publicly burned their magical books (Acts 19:18–20). Actions like these would later give Christians the reputation of being atheists.

The most famous incident at Ephesus, however, was the riot caused by the souvenir makers, led by a certain Demetrius the silversmith. There was a full scale riot, as the crowds pushed their way into the great open air theatre and howled out "Great is Artemis of the Ephesians" for about two hours non-stop (Acts 19:23–24). It was a highly dangerous situation. Two of Paul's friends were seized, but fortunately there were some cool heads among the civic leaders. Some, perhaps secret sympathizers with Paul, managed to prevent the fiery little apostle from confronting the crowd (Acts 19:35–41). He must have been a remarkable man, this town clerk. With a mixture of soothing words about the image of the great goddess, suggestions of legal action in court if people had grievances and a sharp warning that the Roman authorities didn't take kindly to rioting (people knew that the army might be sent in to restore order), he calmed down the situation. Paul left soon after, and we do not know if he ever went to Ephesus again.

– Adapted from What happened next?, *Mike Smith*

MONEY FOR OLD RELIGION

Pilgrims came to Ephesus from all parts of the Mediterranean. And there were hordes of people making a very good living from them. Little models of the temple were made; the cheaper ones were pottery, but deluxe versions were made in silver. All for the veneration of "the great goddess" Artemis, the many breasted mother goddess. Ephesus was also famous for its religious/magical literature. Magical texts, predictions of the future and kinds of mystical writing were readily available. In fact, Ephesus grammata (Ephesian writings) were famous throughout the Greco-Roman world. Even the Jewish community got involved. The secret and very sacred name of Jehovah was considered a very potent spell. No doubt strict rabbis would have disapproved, but there was ready money to be made. You could put it about that you were

a Jewish high priest and gullible crowds would come flocking for the latest exotic magical spell. Exorcism was also practised, as well as spell making and curses and all manner of other ritualistic mumbo-jumbo. And it was into this ferment of superstition that the Apostle Paul had come, and founded a flourishing church.

– Adapted from What Happened Next?, *Mike Smith*

Ephesus was a notorious centre of pagan superstition. It was famous for the Ephesian letters, amulets and charms which were supposed to be infallible remedies for sickness, to bring children to those who were childless and to ensure success in any undertaking – and people came from all over the world to buy them.

– William Barclay

Jesus writes to his church

STUDY GUIDE   DAY THREE

"You were ever of one mind with the apostles in the power of Jesus Christ."
– *Bishop Ignatius of Antioch, writing to the church at Ephesus while on his way to martyrdom in Rome*

Ephesus

These are the words of him who holds the seven stars in his right hand and walks among the seven golden lampstands:

Rev 2:1

"When people put up barriers between church and church, they do what Christ never does."
– *William Barclay*

50

Encouragement for the Ephesians – Christ is truly great

The Ephesian Christians were living in a culture where:

- Occultism was rife – a constant reminder of the power of pagan gods
- Promiscuity was widespread – which would have made them feel that they were swimming against the tide in their desire to live holy lives
- Life was cheap and disposable – babies were often found dumped on the city rubbish tip
- It seemed that other people held all the power – the prevailing notion that life was in the hands of a distant government that held sway over their lives.

They must have felt overwhelmed by pressure from outside the church, and the invasion of heretics and relational tensions within the church. They felt powerless, disenfranchised. But Christ writes to encourage them that he, as it were, knows their address.

His message of encouragement to them is threefold:

- I'm in charge
- I know what you're walking through
- You are held tight in my hand.

His words of comfort answer two fearful questions:

Does the emperor rule?

When Emperor Domitian's young son died in AD83, Domitian proclaimed him to be a god and Domitia (the child's mother) the queen of heaven. Coins were stamped portraying the child playing with stars.

Christ rules.

Christ himself is seen as King of heaven and earth, walking in the midst of his Church, holding the seven stars in his hand (see also John 10:28). The Greek word here is *kratein*, a strong word suggesting that the churches are firmly gripped in his hand.

Have we been deserted?

With gathering pressure, the believers in Ephesus may have felt a sense of abandonment.

Emperor Domitian

VISION OF MARVELLOUS POWER

Take this picture and look at it again and again until the vision holds you in its marvellous power.

His head and his hair white like wool, his purity and his eternity;

his eyes like a flame of fire, his intimate knowledge, penetrating and piercing;

his feet like burnished brass, signifying the procedure of strength and purity;

his voice like the voice of many waters, a concord of perfect tones;

in his hand seven stars, his administrative right, power and protection;

from his mouth a sharp two-edged sword, keen and accurate verdicts concerning his people;

his whole countenance as the sun, creating day, flashing light, bathing all the landscape with beauty.

– *G. Campbell Morgan*

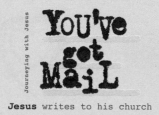

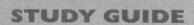
✉ **Ephesus**

I know your deeds, your hard work and your perseverance.

Rev 2:2

"In the modern church, qualities such as perseverance and loyalty are in short supply. In an age of instant coffee, instant glue and instant bank loans, we don't take easily to the pain of sticking to unglamorous tasks, or developing a discipline in prayer. But as Samuel Chadwick said, 'All God's things are grown things. He is never in the ready-made business.'"

– Stephen Travis

✉ **Ephesus**

I know that you cannot tolerate wicked men, that you have tested those who claim to be apostles but are not, and have found them false.

Rev 2:2

After the Gospel, David Winter, BRF

Christ knows. Far from rejecting them, Christ is walking among them, seeing them clearly with 20/20 vision: He sees the hidden works, not just as a patrolling detective, but is aware of their struggles and works. To every one of the seven churches he says, "I know" (see also Matt 28:19).

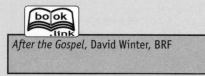 **WE ARE IT!**
virus warning Not only is our church in the hand of Christ; the whole church is in his hand.

Press to reply

Do we have a tendency to think of our church, or our denomination, as being in the palm of his hand – whereas other churches might be not quite so secure? Why do we sometimes think this way?

More encouragement for the Ephesians

The Church at Ephesus was very strong in a number of key areas:

Well done, you've persevered

We can't be sure of the exact nature of the struggles that the Ephesian Christians had walked through; most likely it was the ongoing experience of subtle opposition that had the potential to wear them down; challenges that we face today. For the Ephesians these challenges might have included:

☒ Ethical compromises: later churches would prescribe that any believer who wanted to be baptized would not be allowed to participate in artistic work that involved making pagan images – making it difficult for some disciples of Christ to find work

☒ Christian slaves might have unsympathetic masters

☒ Christian women married to unbelieving husbands who had little or no sympathy or respect for new kingdom priorities embraced by their wives

☒ Social apartheid: some of the congregation had publicly set fire to their occultist bric-à-brac (Acts 19:17–20) . They had literally burnt their bridges. Family, friends and business associates may not have understood and were holding them at arms length.

Well done, you've tested false doctrine

In his farewell speech to the elders at Ephesus (Acts 20:29), Paul prophetically warned them: "After I leave, savage wolves will come in among you." A number of heresies threatened the doctrinal purity

Ephesus town hall on the Street of Curates, where the Asiatic caravan route ended in a great Roman export centre.

THEO
LINK

NICOLAITAN HERESY

According to early church traditions, the false doctrines the Ephesians ran up against came about by a misunderstanding of a church deacon named Nicolaus. The book of Acts says he was a convert to Judaism who became a Christian and was later appointed as a church deacon by the apostles. According to Clement of Alexandria (c.150–c.215), this man had an attractive young wife, and the apostles accused Nicolaus of jealousy because of her beauty. To prove he was not a jealous man, Nicolaus offered his wife to any one of them who would have her, and he became one of the first ascetic Christians (a case of misguided zeal). Of course, they did not take him up on the offer or they would have been worse than what they accused him of. After this, according to tradition, Nicolaus began preaching that "the flesh must be treated with contempt." He renounced all desire in the belief that yielding to pleasure was a distraction from serving God. The sect that claimed his name deliberately misinterpreted this famous statement, however, as a license to get fat, get drunk and practice promiscuity. After all, if this body of flesh wasn't important, what did it matter what you did with it?

Irenaeus (c.130–c.200) says of the Nicolaitans that they lived lives of 'unrestrained indulgence' (Against Heresies, 1.26.3). The Apostolic Constitutions (6:8), written between 350 and 380, describe the Nicolaitans as "shameless in uncleanness." Clement of Alexandria says; "They abandon themselves to pleasure like goats, leading a life of self-indulgence." But he acquits Nicolaus of all blame. The Nicolaitans obviously taught loose living.

Ephesus

But you have this in your favour:
You hate the practices of the
Nicolaitans, which I also hate.

Rev 2:6

"You all live according to the
truth, and no heresy has a home
among you; indeed, you do not
so much as listen to anyone of
they speak of anything except
concerning Jesus Christ in truth."

– *Bishop Ignatius of Antioch, writing to Ephesians*

 Ephesus

You have persevered and endured
hardship for my name, and have
not grown weary.

Rev 2:3

 Ephesus

Yet I hold this against you: You
have forsaken your first love.

Rev 2:4

of the church, including Jews who tried to convince new Christians they must become entangled in the demands of the law in order to be saved, and at the other extreme teachers who tried to turn the newfound freedom of the gospel into a license for sin. Because the Ephesians were situated on a major trade route and highway to Rome they were more at the mercy of these itinerant trouble makers. R.C. Trench notes that "a whole rabble of evil doers" was liable to descend upon the church there. Some itinerant ministries were primarily interested in 'fleecing the flock' or 'getting free bed and breakfast' (Didache 11:6, 12:1–4). But the Ephesians had successfully put the false teaching of the Nicolaitans to the test.

Well done, you've worked hard

The risen Christ praises their 'work'. The word is *kopos*, a favourite in the New Testament. Tryphena, Tryphosa and Persis all 'work hard' in the Lord (Rom 16:12). The one thing Paul claims is that he has worked harder than all (1 Cor 15:10). He fears lest the Galatians slip back and he has 'wasted' his efforts (Gal 4:11). In each case – and there are many others – the word is either *kopos* or *kopian* (verb). The special characteristic of these words is that they describe the kind of work that is extremely demanding. So there were many things to be encouraged about – but they were lacking in one major area.

Could do better: the urgent call to love – "you have lost your first love"

The rebuke that Christ brings does not imply that there was no love in the hearts of the Ephesian believers – but rather that they did not love with the intensity that had been theirs at first (*protos*). The call to love was not an option, as if faithfulness, hard work and doctrinal purity were sufficient – they were threatened with severe judgment if they failed to repent.

Christ affirms that love – and not just theological orthodoxy – is the true measure of maturity for his followers. But what exactly does the phrase 'first love' refer to?

- ☒ It has often been understood to mean a first love, or first flush of enthusiasm for God.
- ☒ Most commentators now see this as a rebuke for a lack of love in the Ephesians' relationships among themselves
- ☒ Some (like G.K. Beale) say the issue was a lack of willingness to share the gospel with outsiders, and therefore love for the lost was lacking.

DIDACHE – A DEFINITION

Didache – the Teaching of the Twelve Apostles, was written between AD80 and AD120. An authoritative writing regarded as Scripture by early Christians, it contains 22 quotations from Matthew and has references to Luke, John, Acts, Romans, Thessalonians and 1 Peter. It speaks of "the gospel" as a written document and became part of the official New Testament canon.

– from Halley's Bible Handbook

WORKING FOR GOD – A VIEW FROM CLEMENT OF ROME

Clement was one of the earliest Christian writers, born at about the time of the crucifixion of Jesus and so contemporary with many of the first Christians. He became known as the bishop (or overseer) of the church at Rome, which seems to have had from earliest times some role of seniority among the churches. His letter was written towards the end of the first century, which means that it is in the immediate post-apostolic era. Typically, Clement saw the issues facing the world at that time as a clash between darkness and light, good and evil, Satan and Christ. He was also sharply aware of the danger of divisions and splits in the Church and of the need for the Christians to hold fast to the faith in a culture that was highly suspicious of 'alien' cults and philosophies. The church was fearing persecution because of the assassination of the emperor, Domitian. For Clement, the answer was to hold fast to the truth, to the church and, above all, to Christ. His letter is steeped in the Old Testament Scriptures.

There's nothing wrong with work. After all, even the Lord and Architect of the universe not only 'worked' on his creation, but derived pleasure and satisfaction from it – he 'saw that it was good'. For his own delight he created the skies and set the stars in order, divided the dry land from the waters and marked out their boundaries. His work continued as he gave life to the animals that live on the land, as well as to the creatures that live in the waters. Finally, to complete his labours, he formed man from the dust of the ground, shaping him in his own likeness. Only then, his work ended, did he pause, satisfied, to rest and to give the creation his blessing.

So if God himself could find joy and satisfaction in his work – work well done, work completed – so may we. In fact, we already have his command to put all our energy and enthusiasm into our work, doing it 'heartily, as though for the Lord'. We already have his command – now we have added his example. Let's spare no effort to obey his will for us where our work is concerned.

There is never any need to feel ashamed of the money you earn, provided you do indeed earn it! But if you don't – if you're a half hearted, unreliable employee – then, of course, you'll probably be embarrassed every time you meet your 'boss'.

For Christians the 'boss' is God. That's why we should do our work with all our hearts and souls. We are answerable to him for the quality of our work – and it is simply impossible to avoid meeting the Lord! 'Look,' says Scripture, 'the Lord is approaching, bringing rewards, to pay each as his work deserves.'

So he tells us not to be lazy or inefficient in any piece of work we do. No one who does his or her work 'before the Lord' will miss his or her reward. Think of the angels, that vast company of heaven, spending every moment in his service, waiting instantly to obey each of his commands. 'Ten thousand times ten thousand stand before him and thousands upon thousands serve him, crying, "Holy, holy, holy, Lord God of hosts: all creation is full of his glory".'

That should be a picture for us of our work: our daily work, done for his glory; and our work of praise and witness in the church, as we are gathered together in perfect unity to do his will.

– Adapted from After the Gospel, *David Winter*

In reality, it's a biblical impossibility to separate these three elements of love anyway:

- ✉ If we love God, then we will love one another (1 John 4:20)
- ✉ Love for each other without God at the heart is impossible for the fruit of the Spirit is love (Gal 5:22)
- ✉ Those who love God will love the world he loves (John 3:16).

Because most commentators see A LACK OF LOVE AMONG THE EPHESIANS as the primary issue, we shall spend more time examining the call to the church to be a loving community, and the need for us to love God and love the lost.

The cell church movement has encouraged churches to embrace a threefold mission statement – the call to love God, love one another, and love the lost. This provides a helpful framework for us today.

Loving God

Paul wrote to the Ephesians, "Grace to all who love our Lord Jesus Christ with an undying love" (Eph 6:24). Now thirty years have passed. Is their love for Christ still alive?

In considering loving God, we should know that love for God is:

- ✉ a love in response to the knowledge that we are loved first by God himself (1 John 4:19)
- ✉ not to be measured in romantic-type feelings or the inconsistency of our emotional condition (1 John 4:16)
- ✉ frequently expressed in thanksgiving and gratitude daily (Eph 5:4, Phil 4:6, 1 Tim 4:4)
- ✉ maintained by a conscious commitment to live abiding lives (John 15:4)
- ✉ truly demonstrated by obedience and faithfulness (1 John 2:4, John 14:15, 24)
- ✉ expressed in warm-hearted worship, whatever the particular style or expression (John 4:23–24)
- ✉ to be found where there is a genuine willingness to allow Christ to reign and rule in his church, which demands that we negotiate God-ordained change rather than demanding our own way (Matt 16:18)
- ✉ leading us to true holiness and purity – the reverse of the Nicolaitan heresy of lawlessness (1 John 3:3)
- ✉ incomplete and worthless unless it is also expressed in loving the sister or brother that we can see (1 John 4:20, Matt 25:35–40)

"Being relevant is not only about believing and behaving; it's also about loving. It not only means fulfilling the Great Commission to reach and teach others; it also means fulfilling the Great Commandment to love God and people. It is essential to take a biblical stand and teach the truth on all the right issues. But without a passionate heart of love for God and others, such efforts are as appealing to people as noisy gongs and clanging cymbals. All across church history we find those who, like the Pharisees, inflicted much pain and hindered the ministry of the gospel in the name of believing and behaving correctly. The Crusades, the Inquisition, the defence of slavery ... the bombing of abortion clinics – all were done in the name of 'truth'. Where did these people fail? They missed the heart of love behind the truths and in doing so they actually perverted the truth. They were obsessed with the mission while oblivious to the heart of love that is to motivate the mission."
– David Fergusson

"Your feelings are not a barometer of your spirituality."
– Adrian Plass

LOVING GOD – AND THE PEOPLE HE LOVES

Who can explain the bond of God's love? Who is able to tell its greatness and its beauty? Truly, words cannot describe the heights to which the love of God can lift us.

Love unites us to God. 'Love covers a multitude of sins.' Love bears all things, is patient and kind. There is nothing corrupt about love, and nothing proud. Love never sets out to divide or to undermine good order. Love does everything in a spirit of unity. God's chosen people are made perfect, and without love nothing is pleasing to God.

In love the Master welcomes us. For love, and love alone, by the will of the Father, Jesus shed his blood for us, giving his flesh for our flesh and his life for ours.

So let anyone who claims to know the love of Christ prove it by doing what he commands. That is the test of love: 'if you love me, keep my commandments.'

– Clement of Rome

Journeying with Jesus

You've got Mail

Jesus writes to his church

STUDY GUIDE   DAY THREE

"Have you tried to start 'feeling love' again? Have you ever fallen out of love and then tried to will the old feelings back again? It does not work. Jesus does not tell us to feel love. What does work? Start doing the loving things you did when you were in love. If it is your [partner], start dating again. If it is your God, start praising and thanking, believing and trusting, rejoicing and worshipping. You can behave your way into feeling much faster than you can feel your way into believing."

– *Neil T. Anderson*

Setting your church free, Neil T. Anderson, Regal Books

"Loss of first love ... more likely means that the first fine rapture of love for the brotherhood had gone. In the first days the members of the church at Ephesus had really loved each other; dissension had never reared its head; the heart was ready to kindle and the hand was ready to help. But something had gone wrong. It may well have been that heresy hunting had killed love and orthodoxy had been achieved at the price of fellowship. When that happens, orthodoxy has cost too much. All the orthodoxy in the world will never take the place of love."

– *William Barclay*

virus ⚠ warning 🕷 **LACK OF LOVE**
Where loving God is not the central focus in our lives, our Christianity degenerates into lifeless activism; the church becomes a loose affiliation of friends rather than an agape community; evangelism becomes a chore that we choose to ignore rather than a passion born of love for God the evangelist.

Press to reply

Why do new Christians often demonstrate such vitality and open passion for God – which can fade and die? Does familiarity have to breed contempt?

Love one another

John was for many years the bishop at Ephesus – and the church there seemed to emulate John's two best-known character traits. He was a man capable of great tenderness and love, and yet could also act like a "son of thunder", for whom love could be eclipsed by hot anger. Had the church become so passionate for truth that it had become hard and unrighteously intolerant – a problem that John had occasionally met in his own life (see Mark 3:17, Luke 9:54–55)?

Wanted: a loving church

Our culture is suffering from techno-isolation – people are hungry for the warmth of community and friendship. But rapid change, household fragmentation and increased mobility are contributing factors to loneliness being the epidemic of the third millennium:

- The most popular 'soaps' on television are all centred around the dynamics of life, sometimes very mundane life, in a community
- The 'docu-soap' is increasingly popular at the expense of action drama; docu-soaps provide fly-on-the-wall views of mundane domesticity – the life of an airport cleaner, for example – and are devoured with great interest
- Are programmes like Big Brother and Survivor more than mass voyeurism?
- Internet chat forums provide opportunity for interaction and relationship – getting information from the information super-highway is not enough
- The continuing popularity of the pub in Britain, despite the vast array of electronic entertainment available; together with the revival of cinema when it was thought the video player would destroy it

58

LIKE LEADER, LIKE CHURCH

The character of the church came to reflect the character of its leader. The two sides of the John of the New Testament – an apostle of love, yet a 'son of thunder' are seen again, interestingly enough, in two stories that have been handed down concerning his later years at Ephesus: on the one hand his refusal to stay under the same roof as the heretic Cerinthus, and on the other his reduction of all his message to a sermon of one sentence, which in extreme old age he used to repeat at every church meeting: "Little children, love one another". We can tell from Acts and Ephesians that the early church there was likewise characterized by both love and zeal. ... Paul could write of her "love towards all the saints" (Eph 1:15)... but some years later, as John writes, her zeal is undiminished; her works, toils, and patient endurance are all commended, and especially the value she places on sound doctrine ... but in her keenness for the truth, the church at Ephesus has lost her love, "the one quality without which all others are worthless."

– Adapted from The Message of Revelation, *Michael Wilcock, BST*

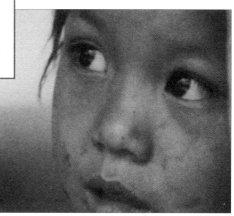

WE REALLY DO NEED EACH OTHER

In the past standardized congregations required everyone to sit, stand and kneel at the same time. They were instructed what to think through the sermon, and it was expected that they would all believe roughly the same. People who did not fit the mould left. The evacuation of the church since the 1950s involved a flight from this uniform approach.

Some people have taken refuge in highly individualistic forms of spirituality, spirituality that is practised in groups of one. But it is not easy for spirituality to flourish when you are on your own. It can help to pray with other people, whether the prayers are formal, extempore or silent. A group in prayer creates an atmosphere which encourages each member to pray. Being with others aids worship too. As other people come into the presence of God you are drawn along with them. Learning about the faith with others provides stimulation and encouragement. The larger entity creates a context in which the individual can encounter God. Take away that context, and it becomes harder to develop your spirituality ... while there is certainly a place for personal prayer and study, there is little future for solo-spirituality done purely on your own.

– Changing World, Changing Church, Michael Moynagh

You've got Mail

Journeying with Jesus

Jesus writes to his church

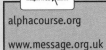

The Message of Revelation, Michael Wilcock, BST

> "This new church ministered to one another. They loved each other, confessed their sins to one another, served one another and carried others' burdens. It is difficult to imagine them 'congregating', sitting in rows, looking at the back of one another's heads."
>
> – *Michael Mack*, The Synergy Church

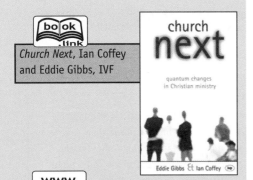

Church Next, Ian Coffey and Eddie Gibbs, IVF

church next

quantum changes in Christian ministry

Eddie Gibbs & Ian Coffey

www
http//web link

alphacourse.org

www.message.org.uk

The Great Commandment Principle, David Fergusson, Tyndale House

- Half a million different types of support groups (such as Alcoholics Anonymous) exist in the USA
- The phenomenal impact of Alpha (over a million have completed the course in the UK), which is a relational, interactive method of exploring the claims of Christ

virus ⚠ warning

RELATIONSHIPS BEFORE PROGRAMME
If we are to meet the felt needs of our culture, we will not do so simply by offering people the opportunity to attend services – even innovative, creative, entertaining and exciting services. They are looking for genuine friendship and belonging.

Press to reply

† What would happen if your minister suggested cancelling the Sunday morning communion service and having a barbecue instead?

† Is communion actually communal in your church – or an exercise in solitary reflection?

† Is your church at ease with laughter?

† How much time do you spend with people from your church outside the services?

Elements of loving churches

Love can become a clichéd, sentimentalized idea; rather than a practical reality. Some of the characteristics of a loving church are:

- fellowship – a desire and commitment to be together (Acts 2:42)
- opportunities for prayer for one another (James 5:16, Luke 22:32, Eph 6:18, Rom 12:12, Col 1:9, 1 Thess 5:17)
- a culture of reality and confession (James 5:16, Matt 5:24)
- a sense of encouragement (Heb 3:13, Eph 4:16)
- burden-bearing at an emotional and practical level (Eph 4:32, Phil 2:4, Gal 6:2, 1 Thess 5:14, Rom 15:1)
- willingness to engage in conflict negotiation (Eph 4:2)
- investment into time together outside of services – hospitality (Matt 25:35, Rom 12:13, Gal 6:10, Col 4:10, Phm 22, 1 Tim 3:2, Titus 1:8, 1 Pet 4:9, Heb 13:2)
- Sharing of financial and other resources (Rom 12:13, 1 Tim 6:18, Heb 13:16)

A LOVING COMMUNITY

LESSONS FROM THE BAR

The neighbourhood bar is possibly the best counterfeit there is for the fellowship Christ wants to give his church. It's an imitation dispensing liquor instead of grace, escape rather than reality, but it is a permissive, accepting and inclusive fellowship. It is unshockable. It is democratic. You can tell people secrets and they usually don't tell others or even don't want to. The bar flourishes not because most people are alcoholics, but because God has put into the human heart the desire to know and be known, to love and be loved.

– *Bruce Larson*

ROLLING IN THE AISLES

Unfeigned, practical love has a magnetic power far more effective than evangelistic programs which depend almost entirely on verbal communication. People do not want to hear us talk about love, they want to experience how Christian love really works. The question of whether there is much laughter in church has a correlation with the quality of the church and its growth. Interestingly enough, aspects like this find little mention in church growth literature.

– *Christian A. Schwarz*

HOLY JOE'S AND OTHERS

Meeting in a pub is a way that some congregations have sought to be earthed in the consumer world. In the mid-1990s, "Cornerstone" was meeting in the 'Odd One Out', a pub run by Christian landlords in Colchester. One of its leaders introduced it as 'open to all who are searching spiritually yet find conventional churches too daunting'

Dave Tomlinson's Holy Joe's is a worshipping group that meets in the upper room of a pub in a cloud of cigarette and pipe smoke and with drinks served from the bar. Holy Joe's attracts disillusioned former evangelicals, as well as seekers who are not yet prepared to darken the doorway of any church but who want a place to go where they feel comfortable and can raise honest

questions and demand honest answers. Tomlinson's background and spiritual pilgrimage started in the Christian Brethren and went to the House Church movement, where he became a prominent leader. He later left it to adopt a controversial 'post-evangelical' position, which he articulated in his book *The Post Evangelical*, published in 1995.

The 'Group' in Oxford has met on Thursday nights for over five years. They eat together in different homes, and punctuate the meal with a liturgy, songs, prayers and lots of laughter. They often discuss current affairs, and the relevance or otherwise of faith. Admittedly they are mainly Christians, but might groups of non-churchgoers do something similar, allowing worship, prayer and study to evolve at the group's pace as it grows into faith?

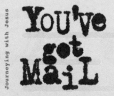

You've got Mail

Journeying with Jesus

Jesus writes to his church

"You have given up loving each other as you did at first."

– Rev 2:4 (Moffatt translation)

"Pure doctrine alone, as countless examples illustrate, does not induce growth. A church, regardless of how orthodox its dogma and view of Scripture, can hardly expect to experience growth, as long as its members do not learn to live their faith with contagious enthusiasm and to share it with others. Wherever a 'defence of orthodoxy' replaces the expression of a passionate faith in Christ, a false paradigm is at work."

– Christian A. Schwarz

"People still want groups, ... this provides fabulous opportunities for evangelism. For community is at the heart of church. When someone joins church, hopefully they join a community where they will be loved, in which they can find a framework for life, which will help them nurture their spirituality and to which they can make a contribution, boosting their self-esteem. Church should be superbly placed to meet the longing to belong. But to do so the church will need to think more imaginatively about what it means to be a community."

– Michael Moynagh

book link

Natural Church Development, Christian A. Schwarz

Press to reply

Do you need to go back from Spring Harvest and repair any relationships in your family, workplace or local church?

Growing in love

- Realise that love is a gift of God (Gal 5:22, 1 Thess 4:9, Rom 5:5), but love will be tested (Eph 4:2)
- Be filled with the Holy Spirit (Eph 5:18, Col 3:8–17, Eph 4:22–5:2). A key to closeness in our relationships is our own daily closeness to God
- Value people by seeing them in Christ (Phil 2:29, Rom 16:2) – they are people for whom Christ died (Rom 14:15, 1 Cor 8:11, Rom 15:7) – they are those in whom Christ lives (Acts 9, Matt 25:31) – they are those through whom one day Christ will reign (1 Cor 6:3, 2 Tim 2:12, Matt 19:28, Luke 22:9, Rom 8:17)
- Remember to forget (Matt 18:21); bitterness feeds on the inability to let go of hurts
- Realise that love is practical (1 John 3:18, James 2:14-26, John 13:34) and is not just about words (John 13:1)
- Be realistic – people are living busier lives, and it is a challenge to develop and maintain more than one or two meaningful friendships, as well as balancing family and work
- Realise that love and niceness are not the same thing. God disciplines those whom he loves (Heb 12:6). Jesus loved his disciples to the end (John 13:1), but he still rebuked them with the truth (Matt 16:23)

Press to reply

There has been a lot of discussion in Christian circles about the issue of homosexuality in the last twelve months. Some say love means:

† Acceptance and dialogue
† A refusal to judge

While others insist:

† Dialogue implies that we are diluting the truth of Scripture
† Love demands that the truth be told

How can we balance truth and love in this issue?

LOOKING CLOSER AT LOVE

'Love' can easily descend into clichéd sentimentality; or we can just assume we love one another, because we have a vague affection. Just what are some of the essential elements of love?

1.   Comfort

Giving strength and hope; easing grief or pain; consoling – The God of all comfort, who comforts us in all our troubles, so that we can comfort those in any trouble. (2 Cor 1:3–4, Rom 12:15)

2.   Attention

Taking thought of another and conveying appropriate interest and concern; entering another's world – "The members of the body should have the same care for one another." (1 Cor 12:25, NASB)

3.   Acceptance

Deliberate and ready reception with a favourable response; receiving willingly; regarding as good and proper – "Accept one another, then, just as Christ accepted you, in order to bring praise to God" (Rom 15:7)

4.   Appreciation

Recognizing with gratitude; communicating with words and gestures personal gratefulness for another person; praising – "I praise you" (1 Cor 11:2)

5.   Support

Coming alongside and gently helping to carry a problem or struggle; assisting; providing for – "Carry each other's burdens, and in this way you will fulfill the law of Christ" (Gal 6:2)

6.   Encouragement

Urging forward and positively persuading toward a goal; inspiring with courage, spirit or hope; stimulating – "Therefore encourage one another and build each other up" (1 Thess 5:11)

7.   Affection

Communicating care and closeness through physical touch and affirming words – "Having thus a fond affection for you, we were well-pleased to impart to you not only the gospel of God but also our own lives" (1 Thess 2:8 NASB)

8.   Respect

Valuing and regarding highly: conveying great worth; esteeming, honouring – "Show proper respect to everyone" (1 Pet 2:17)

9.   Security

Freedom from harm, danger and fear; putting beyond hazard of losing, want or deprivation – "Perfect love drives out fear" (1 John 4:18)

10.   Approval

Affirming as satisfactory; giving formal sanction to; expressing a favourable opinion of – "Anyone who serves Christ in this way is pleasing to God and approved by men" (Rom 14:18)

– Adapted from The Great Commandment Principle, *David Fergusson, Tyndale House*

Journeying with Jesus

You've got MaiL

Jesus writes to his church

"If our church fellowship is not the kind of company where a person who has failed feels welcome and loved, the kind of place where he can face up to life again and begin to work his way back to the standards and patterns from which he has stumbled, then our church is denying the very spirit of its Lord no matter how orthodox its testimony."

– Bruce Milne

We Belong Together – The Meaning Of Fellowship, Bruce Milne, Inter Varsity Press

Church Next, Eddie Gibbs and Ian Coffey, IVP

church **next**

quantum changes in Christian ministry

Eddie Gibbs & Ian Coffey

Love the lost

We need to love the lost – this is a subject worthy of detailed thought and action. We must remind ourselves that a loving community that does not love those outside of itself has become a homely, irrelevant club, and is refusing to emulate and reflect the passion in God's heart for the lost, who so urgently need to know that they are loved.

There is no doubt about the intensity and extent of the Father's concern so eloquently and succinctly expressed in John's gospel (3:16). Note also Jesus' expression of that concern. He wept over an unresponsive Jerusalem (Matt 23:37). Notice the intensity of concern that characterized Paul's ministry in Ephesus (Acts 20:31). He also felt just as intensely about his own people (Rom 9:1–5). Contrast Paul's passion with Jonah's disregard for the citizens of Nineveh as he sat on a vantage point overlooking the city in a sulking attitude of judgmental detachment (Jonah 4:1–3). Dwight L. Moody expressed his own mission in the dramatic terms of a sea rescue. "I look upon this world as a wrecked vessel. Its ruin is getting nearer and nearer. God said to me, 'Moody, here is the lifeboat – rescue as many as you can before the crash comes'!" An older generation of evangelicals spoke of a passion for souls. Due to the shallowness of our spirituality and the nervousness we feel in the face of a secularised and pluralistic world, this passion seems to have largely evaporated. It is one of the most disturbing characteristics of the contemporary evangelical church.

When faced with the challenges of a lost, confused and sometimes hostile world, the church may respond in:

- ✉ Judgmental isolation – "The world is rushing to hell, and we want nothing to do with it"
- ✉ Protective separation – "The world is dangerous, and we must separate ourselves from it in order to live holy lives"
- ✉ Missionary engagement – "The world is a dark place that needs the light that Christ calls the church to be. A cloistered holiness isn't worth much anyway."

Press to reply

Which of these three responses describes you – and your church?

ALL I NEED IS LOVE

Self-centeredness in human hearts and individualism in contemporary culture create a loneliness that cries out for relief. James Baldwin captured this aching longing in a poignant description of a young man:

"The joint, as Fats Waller would have said, was jumping. ... And during the last set, the saxophone player took off on a terrific solo. He was a kid from some insane place like Jersey City or Syracuse. But somewhere along the line he had discovered he could say it with a saxophone. He stood there, wide-legged, humping the air, filling his narrow chest, shivering in the rags of his twenty odd years, and screaming through the horn, "Do you love me?" "Do you love me?" "Do you love me?" And again, "Do you love me?" "Do you love me?" "Do you love me?" The same phrase unbearable, endlessly and variously repeated with all the force the kid had... . The question was terrible and real. The boy was blowing with his lungs and guts out of his own short past; and somewhere in the past in gutters and gang fights ... in the acrid room, behind marijuana or the needles, under the smell in the precinct basement, he had received a blow from which he would never recover, and this no one wanted to believe. Do you love me? Do you love me? Do you love me? The men on the stand stayed with him cool and at a little distance, adding and questioning. But each man knew that the boy was blowing for everyone of them."

The church exists to answer that young man's question. By its proclamation of the gospel it points to the love of God in Jesus Christ and says, "Yes, you are loved, loved more than you can imagine, loved by a God who will never let you go." And because the church, too, lives by and in this love, because it draws its life from the Holy One, it becomes a company of prodigal lovers.

– Adapted from The Trivialization of God, *Donald W. McCullough*

THE CHURCH THAT LOVES THE LOST

In *Church Next*, Ian Coffey and Eddie Gibbs point to twelve indicators of a mission-centred church – a people that genuinely love the lost:

1 It is a church that proclaims the gospel.
2 It is a community where all members are involved in learning to become disciples of Jesus.
3 The Bible is normative in the life of the church.
4 The church understands itself as different from the world because of its participation in the life, death and resurrection of its Lord.
5 The church seeks to discern God's specific missional vocation for the entire community and for all its members.
6 Christians behave Christianly toward one another.
7 The church is a community that practises reconciliation.
8 People within the community hold themselves accountable to one another in love.
9 The church practises hospitality.
10 Worship is the central act by which the community celebrates with joy and thanksgiving both God's presence and God's promised future.
11 The church is a community that has a vital public witness.
12 There is a recognition that the church itself is an incomplete expression of the reign of God

Journeying with Jesus

You've got MaiL

Jesus writes to his church

"Christian love is the final apologetic."

– *Francis Schaeffer*

The Church at the End of the Twentieth Century, Francis Schaeffer, Norfolk Press

www.kings-church-eastbourne.org.uk

www.communigate.co.uk/york/
saturdaykidsclub/

"What is life if we have not life together?"

– *T.S. Eliot*

"A true relationship with Christ will mean a new relationship with his people. We cannot be related to Christ without being at the same time related to His body, the church, the universal company of all who are renewed by the Holy Spirit."

– *Bruce Milne*

"Building relationships was an intentional, aggressive agenda for Christ. He spent time with his disciples (John 3:22). He lived by the principle that people respond when we reach out to them."

– *Dann Spader*

www.icthus.org.uk

A church for the lost

Archbishop William Temple famously said: "The church is the only organization that exists for the benefit of its non-members." This is perhaps the ideal, but if we are to ensure that it becomes reality rather than a vague aspiration, we must consider how the church:

- Negotiates change
- Spends its money and uses its buildings
- Knows its community
- Is prepared to venture into dark places

Negotiating change

We will not make an impact on those outside of the church by just continuing to do what we have done to this point. Perhaps it's surprising that we Christians, who have signed up for a journey with Jesus, are the ones who find it so difficult to embrace change. But it must be done if we are to be effective. We must commit ourselves to what Bruce Milne calls 'courageous restructuring.' For some churches this may mean a transition to midweek meeting – or designing events for specific people groups.

Why is change so hard for us?

- We feel that the church is a refuge from change rather than an agent of change
- We nurture a belief that our way of doing things has God's particular stamp of approval
- We confuse adaptability with compromise, feeling that changing to meet the needs of our culture is perhaps allowing ourselves to be shaped by the world
- We have a tendency to attach more reverence than is appropriate to service times and styles
- We develop a belief that the church belongs to us rather than to God.

Press to reply

Can you think of an example of radical change your church could embrace in order to love the lost? What reactions would you anticipate if it were to be put into action?

A LOVING COMMUNITY

NEGOTIATING CHANGE

Openness to change is more difficult to measure. Usually we should assume that most institutions and especially churches are resistant to change. Indeed, too much resistance to change causes petrification. If we don't exercise we eventually can't exercise. We often hear the axiom: "Don't change just for change's sake." I'm not sure that is good advice. We have encouraged some change in the constitution of Wooddale Church almost every year since I became the pastor. Recently, after the church's annual meeting, I commented to my secretary, "I feel badly that we didn't make any changes in the constitution this year." She replied, "that's because there is nothing left to change". That's when I said, "Maybe we should start putting it back the way it used to be." Of course I'm not endorsing frivolous or unproductive changes. I am convinced, however, that healthy churches are changing churches. They are willing to take risks, to undertake new projects and programmes that may fail. An executive recruiter once told me about one of his interviewing techniques. He explained that he asks prospective employees to list some of their biggest failures in previous jobs.

He explains that he preferred to hire those who had failed and still had their jobs. He shied away from prospects who couldn't think of significant failures because he knew they weren't risk takers. It is risky to reach out to unbelievers. It changes a church when newcomers are unlike old-timers. God's work is seldom neat, clean, and free of problems. Our world is changing around us. All healthy organisms adapt or die. The same goes for churches. In his book "User Friendly Churches", George Barna explains that successful churches subscribe to a common philosophy: the ministry is not called to fit the church's structure; the structure exists to further effective ministry. That means that when the structure doesn't work, it is changed. Constants must be the Bible and the mission of the church. Everything else is negotiable. Blessed is the church that tries a different style of music, a new approach to evangelism, or adds a Saturday evening service – even if it doesn't work. And blessed is the church that celebrates the risk taking and openness even if the success that was anticipated does not happen.

– Adapted from A Church for the 21st Century, *Leith Anderson*

COURAGEOUS RESTRUCTURING

- Midweek church is likely to involve new types of congregation. In Deptford, southeast London, a group originally from the Ichthus Fellowship runs a children's church on Saturday morning with up to 80 children. The gathering is led by children supported by adults with songs, games and Bible stories. The aim is to do church through a child's eyes, rather than ask children to fit round adult structures. The demands of time and energy on a relatively small group of adults has forced the congregation to meet less often, but it illustrates another way of doing church.
- For many families with young children, shopping on Saturday morning is a nightmare. So why not start a children's congregation involving games, drama, dance, music and Bible stories, with an invitation for parents to drop off their kids and shop in peace? Occasional events could be held for parents, to offer them a taste of church too. The Salvation Army is working with children in one British supermarket. Large scale Saturday morning 'kids clubs' are being run by churches in Liverpool, Eastbourne and many other towns. Could local churches work together to do something similar elsewhere?
- Alpha courses have been held successfully in the Bank of England and in the head offices of some of the corporations in London. Might it make sense to hold more of these courses (and not just in London)? Some could be encouraged to evolve into 'cell' congregations, resourced by a person with oversight over a number of cells. These cells might meet together from time to time in a larger celebration. They could evolve into a cell church.
- At Todmorton in the Pennine foothills, a family communion service is held on Monday afternoons. Children arrive from school after 3.30 for a drink and biscuits before the 4pm service, which lasts half an hour. 'It provides an opportunity for people who really can't get to church on Sunday,' reports the Vicar, Canon Peter Culvert. 'It is family oriented, and because it's simple and accessible to children, it's also simple and accessible for parents. It has brought people into the worshipping life of the church who find Sunday services a bit awesome, a bit wordy and a bit middle class. It's a real growth point.' It attracts 100 or more children and adults compared to Sunday's attendance of around 150.
- In 1995 an Anglican and a Baptist church in Bristol jointly launched a three-monthly 'seeker service' for older people who did not come to church. The services included drama, an interview, two well-known hymns, a secular song on the theme, and tea – loads of it. They discovered three specific needs – a place to belong, a sense of family and a place that is linked with hope for the future. Those who came wanted the seeker services more often. That was not practical, but a small team started a fortnightly Focus group with a simpler programme – generally a speaker, sharing family news, a hymn and some prayer, followed by food. Here was a realistic response to the needs of a specific group of people. Instead of hoping that older people on the fringe would come to established church, church was built round them and their particular needs. Church was 'customised'.

"I know of a church where on certain Sundays half the congregation prepared double lunches and the other half were their guests. And just to make it really impartial the names of the guests were drawn out of a hat! To some this may seem a little artificial. Yet the church concerned was, and remains, renowned for the quality of its fellowship."

– Bruce Milne

The trivialization of God, Donald W. McCullough

Faithworks, Steve Chalke, Kingsway Publications

"Being close to a few people is more important than being popular enough to receive 400 Christmas cards every year."

– Alan McGinnis, The Friendship Factor

"To love at all is to be vulnerable. Love anything, and your heart will certainly be wrung and possibly be broken. If you want to make sure of keeping it intact, you must give your heart to no one. ... Wrap it carefully with hobbies and little luxuries; avoid all entanglements; lock it up safe in a casket of your own selfishness. There it will not be broken: it will become unbreakable, impenetrable, and irredeemable."

– C.S. Lewis

Money and buildings

If we really love, then we will give to the object of our love (James 2:1–4). We must be challenged about the focus of church budgets and stewardship of the thousands of church buildings we collectively own.

- ☒ How much money do we spend on reaching young people?
- ☒ Is our building left idle for most of the week?
- ☒ Do we have a belief that only overtly church activities should happen in 'our' building?
- ☒ Should we be calling for more church buildings that are multi-purpose?
- ☒ How much money is spent on evangelism and the resourcing of evangelists compared to the amount spent on the provision of pastoral care?

Knowing the needs of the community

If we are unaware of the felt needs of the communities of which we are part, we'll provide events, activities and services in which no one is interested. There's a simple way of finding out. We can ask them. Isn't this the heart of the gospel, going to where people are rather than demanding that they come to where we are?

Venturing into dark places

It is easy and comfortable for us to huddle together in the safety and warmth of our church buildings. Mission is founded in going – which means we need to:

- ☒ Release dangerous mission activity, and not slip into an attitude that new approaches to mission are worldly or compromised
- ☒ Make sure that we are 'salting and lighting' our existing friendships in a clear, compassionate life lived for Jesus

To truly be incarnational people, we must be prepared to take risks and venture into the darkest places with the light of the gospel.

- ☒ The 24/7 Prayer initiative recently sent a team of young people to Ibiza, the party capital of Europe, to set up a prayer room in cooperation with local churches. The team distributed thousands of cards to gather prayer requests; they also went into the clubs to pray during the evenings
- ☒ A graduate from Church Army College in Sheffield has been appointed chaplain to the Bournemouth club scene
- ☒ A Spring Harvest worship leader, Dave Bilbrough, has recently

MONEY AND BUILDINGS

Andrew Mawson is the doyen of Britain's 'social entrepreneurs', people with a gift for sparking community development. He is a United Reformed minister in Tower Hamlets, East London. When he started his ministry there were only a handful in the congregation. So he got their permission 'to try anything', and began catalysing one community initiative after another.

In a remarkable story, the number of community groups meeting on church premises grew from one to almost a hundred. The place is now a hive of activity throughout the week. They have built studios and workshops for groups of painters, sculptors, screen-printers, creators of stained glass windows and many others. One of Britain's poorest areas has given birth to one of the country's largest artistic communities – and in an area with over 40 different language groups!

While Andrew was telling me the story, he commented, 'We are committed to building community here. That means that when any group asks to use our buildings, we say to them, "You are very welcome, provided that each year you join with at least one other group on the premises to do something for the local community." That way,' Andrew explained, 'we avoid having lots of isolated groups sharing the building. We start creating real community.'

– Michael Moynagh

WELSH WISDOM

A church in Wales conducted a geodemographic study of their locality. Instead of setting up a church and asking if people wanted to come, they thought they would discover what real needs existed first. One of the results was a plan to plant a congregation in an old people's residential home. The residents will lead it, there will be a Sunday service and the equivalent of house groups will meet during the week. The church involved will provide training, musicians and occasional inputs through testimonies. This will be much more than a service for residents staged by members of the local church, which happens in many places. It will be fully fledged church taking root within the residential home, owned and run by the people there. As it becomes part of the life-blood of the community, it is hoped that non-churchgoers will begin to see it as their congregation and start to attend. The aim is to revitalize the last stages of the residents' lives.

As more people live longer, Britain is rapidly reaching the point where there are more people over 65 than under 16. Just as we train specialists in youth ministry, we need specialists for the new mission field of ministry to older citizens.

> "It is not virtue that can save the world or anyone in it, but love."
> – Archbishop Temple

> "Our presence in a place of need is more powerful than a thousand sermons. Being there is our witness. And until we are, our orthodoxy and doctrine are mere words, our liturgies and gospel choruses ring hollow."
> – Chuck Colson

> "Until the kingdom of God can be demonstrated in our relationships of love with one another, we will having nothing to say to an unbelieving world."
> – David Watson

> "We currently develop churches based on a model of ministry that was developed several hundred years ago, rejecting the fact that the society for which the model was designed no longer exists."
> – George Barna

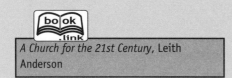

A Church for the 21st Century, Leith Anderson

> "Our wallets have more to do with heaven and also with hell than our hymn books."
> – Helmut Thielicke

Revelation, Jonathan Knight, Sheffield Academic Press

started club evenings in the heart of London's West End theatre land. Performances have been at Jermyn Street Theatre. Dave mixes engaging chat about his life and experiences with secular music and some of his own compositions. The purpose of the evening is to provide an event that Christians can take non-Christian friends to.

Meanwhile, back at Ephesus

Jesus gives words of encouragement to the Ephesians if they will:

- ☒ Remember – a call for corporate reflection
- ☒ Repent – a call for a corporate change of mind
- ☒ Overcome – a call for corporate warfare
- ☒ Do what they used to do – a call for corporate action.

If they refuse to evaluate and take action, Jesus said: "I will come to you and remove your lampstand from its place." This is not a reference to the second coming, because the lampstand of witness will not be needed then – it is a devastating warning that their whole existence as a church is in question.

If, however, they heed the warning, the promise is that they will eat from the tree of life – the promise of eternal reward.

 I'M A BELIEVER
It's clear from this most sobering warning from Christ that belief and mental adherence to his commands don't satisfy him – he is looking for genuine, practical obedience.

RSVP

The city of Ephesus is now gone forever

The harbour was the greatest in Asia. Today there is little left of Ephesus but ruins, and the harbour is six miles from the sea. The coast is a harbourless line of sandy beaches, unapproachable by ship. What was once the Gulf of Ephesus is now a marsh, dense with reeds. The fight with silt from the Cayster was lost. Ephesus vanished from its place of glory as a result.

TRUTH AND LOVE

Imagine – a church, established in 1907 after a notable mission by a famous evangelist, stands in a once-fashionable district of town. Its congregation, drawn from a wide area, are people who appreciate the biblical teaching they receive Sunday by Sunday. The minister does his homework well, and from time to time relates the teaching of scripture carefully to some controversial issue on which they look to him for guidance. Last month it was abortion and genetic research. At Easter he showed in detail why they should reject modern interpretations of the resurrection, which do not accept that Jesus rose physically, leaving the tomb empty. Three years ago they successfully campaigned against the opening of a sex shop near the town centre. This church is buoyant with a strong sense of its mission and its identity as a place where the true gospel is preached.

Yet there is a hardness about it. Strangers who venture inside are mostly ignored, or are questioned about their credentials rather than welcomed warmly. When invited by St. James' Church, which they regard as 'liberal', to share in a march of witness on Good Friday, the church council voted against it for fear of compromising the gospel. Across the road from the church in a run-down building is an advice centre, serving the community of the district. It suffers constantly from lack of resources and people to help. A passion for truth is a dangerous thing unless it is wedded to Christ-like love. The Ephesians have set out to contend for the truth, only to discover that in the course of the battle they have lost the one quality without which all others are worthless. Where love for other people is lost, love for God turns into religious formalism, or fanaticism.

– Stephen Travis

REMOVING THE LAMPSTAND AND THE 'TREE OF LIFE'

Israel had also been symbolized by the lampstand emblem (e.g. Zech 4), but when successive generations renounced their calling to be a light to the nations (Isa 42:6–7, 49:6), God removed them as his light-bearing people and transferred the emblem of that call to the church. That the primary meaning of lampstand is that of witness is confirmed from Rev 11:3–7,10 where 'lampstands' refers to those who are God's 'prophetic witnesses.' Similarly Mark 4:21 and Luke 8:16 say that a lamp is to be put on a lampstand to shine in order to emphasize the witnessing role of those who truly possess God's revelation (cf. also Matt 5:14–16) ... in close connection to the basic formula "if anyone has ears to hear let him hear" (Mark 4:23; Luke 8:8). These two texts also imply that those among God's people who do not shine their light will have their lamps removed (Mark 4:25; Luke 8:18).

The lampstands also generally represent the power of the Spirit, since this is how the lampstand is implicitly identified in Zech 4:6, although ... more precisely ... John views the lamps as the Spirit that burns on the lampstands (the churches), thus empowering them for witness.

The actual wording "I will remove your lampstand from its place" indicates removal of the church as a light of witness to the world, which points to the removal of it before Christ's final coming, since the churches' witness is a relevant activity only before the final advent, not afterward.

– G.K. Beale

If they do not heed, dire consequences are sure and swift. "I will come" is in fact in the present tense: 'I am coming'. John sees it before his eyes. If the church does not heed the injunction, Christ will remove its lampstand, which appears to signify the total destruction of the church. A church can continue only for so long on a loveless course. Without love it ceases to be a church. Its lampstand is removed.

– Leon Morris

The image by which John describes the promise of eternal life is carefully chosen. 'The tree of life, which is in the paradise of God' (Rev 2:7) recalls the description of the Garden of Eden in Gen 2:9. According to Jewish tradition the original perfection of Eden would be restored in the paradise of the future, and the tree of life would feed God's people for ever. But also people in Ephesus would recall that the temple of Artemis stood on what was originally a shrine associated with a sacred tree, and coins of Ephesus frequently portray a tree as an emblem of Artemis. And the temple was surrounded by its own sacred space or 'garden'. So the promise to those who are victorious is a message issued in defiant contrast to the seduction of Artemis and her cult. In Christ there is real security, real hope, in contrast to the attractive claims of seemingly all-powerful contemporary cults and movements.

– Stephen Travis

The Jewish Rabbis taught that in Paradise the tree of life would be there in the middle of heaven, and that all might eat of it. The tree of life is the symbol of immortality, and the meaning of the promise is that, if we live victoriously in the power of the Risen Christ, we have in us the medicine of salvation, the power which defeats death and gives us eternal life.

– William Barclay

 Ephesus

Remember the height from which you have fallen! Repent and do the things you did at first. If you do not repent, I will come to you and remove the lampstand from its place.

Rev 2:5

 Ephesus

To him who overcomes, I will give the right to eat from the tree of life, which is in the paradise of God.

Rev 22:7

"The duty of the church is to be the light of the world, to shine like a light in a dark place. When an electric light bulb loses its power to shine, we throw it away because it has lost the power of doing what it was created to do. Uselessness always invites disaster, and the church which has ceased to shine for Christ has lost the reason for its existence."

– William Barclay

"Many churches today have ceased truly to exist. Their buildings may remain intact, their ministers minister and their congregations congregate, but their lampstand has been removed. The church is plunged into darkness. No glimmer of light radiates from it. It has no light, because it has no love."

– John Stott

"Church and city together have vanished."

– Michael Wilcock

The Ephesian church rallied after Jesus sent them mail

There was:

- Church planting. Churches were planted possibly at Smyrna, Magnesia and Tralles. The leader at Tralles was a young man, indicating that the Ephesian church utilised and released younger people to plant.

- Ongoing loyalty to the message. Around 100 years after the warning was given, the North African Tertullian described the church at Ephesus as the place to go if you wanted to hear the authentic message of Christianity.

But there were long term difficulties:

- Factions and division. Ignatius wrote of some staying away from worship, suggesting that rival factions existed in the city. Some see the statements in other Johannine writings (1 John 2:19, 2 John 7) as evidence of a split in the Ephesian church. One commentator (Aune) suggests there were four splits in the Ephesian church at the beginning of the second century:
  - The church founded by Paul
  - A Jewish-Christian group
  - The heretical Nicolaitan sect
  - A Jewish-Christian group led by John of Patmos

- Majoring on minors. We know there were arguments about which day the church should meet on: Polycrates, a leader of the church at Ephesus, fell out with Victor, the leader of the church at Rome.

In the Middle Ages, a traveller visiting Ephesus said he could find only three Christians and they were "sunken in such ignorance and apathy as scarcely to have heard the names of St. Paul or St. John." The town that was Ephesus is now named Ayasaluk, which means saint theologian and is the name of a church dedicated to John built there in the fifth century.

MAIL FOR YOUR CHURCH

Designed for those in local church leadership, here are some questions to help you think through the implications of today's material for your congregation.

Love one Another – How?

Discuss the seen and the unseen ways it happens.

Let's get down to something practical.

- How do members of the congregation help each other, and is the help too spiritual to be of use?
- Do we listen, or do we always have the answers?
- Do we help or point to someone who can?
- How sure are people that they're loved by God?
- Has the church a tradition that says 'God is Love' or does it say 'God is Love IF …'?

The Welcome

Is there a comfortable welcome?

- Who greets people, and what greets them?
- What help is there if they have young children?
- What help if they are on their own?
- What help if they are elderly?
- What help if they have no church background?
- What do people say as they leave?
- What do people say after they leave?

Your Church's View of Education

We need to grow in love and that involves us in a learning process.

- What have you done so far?
- How do we learn about the faith?
- Do people see learning as a need?
- Do we enable people to learn by doing, and if so in what ways?

- Is there a structured introduction to the faith?
- How can we, if at all, assess the impact or success of learning opportunities?
- Do we learn in small groups, sermon slots or both?
- How do we encourage less committed people to take part in learning opportunities? Is the subject matter relevant? Does it vary or is it predictable?

Now there are many different people coming in to our churches there needs to be consideration of their diverse needs.

The Learning Community

What different groups have you got in your church community? Those who …

- have been within the church for a longer period of time and have had opportunities to learn and grow in the faith.
- have been around a long time but not had an opportunity to continue in the learning process.
- have come to the church community from a Christian journey that involved teaching and growing in the faith.
- have come to the church community with no Christian experience.
- are of different ages.

Identify the main groups in your community and prioritise the most appropriate learning needs.

GETTING THERE

These questions are taken from *Getting There*, a new Spring Harvest book by Ruth Dearnley. It is a book full of questions, to be used by anyone and in any church that's open to fresh challenge and serious thinking about the future.

Some questions are general. Others apply to specific situations and challenges. Some you have asked yourself. Others are asking things in a different way.

Ruth writes; "Questions are crucial to our growing together. We need to ask them and listen to each other's answers – not to force a decision but to

learn what it is that joins us, what we misunderstand and why we choose to go in a particular direction."

Getting There is on sale at Spring Harvest 2002. It is a practical book to be dipped into or worked through over a period of time. It is for all those involved in the leadership and management of the church. It is essential for anyone who wants to ask the questions that inform the way ahead.

Take it home and give it to those who have not been at Spring Harvest so that a church can talk together. You don't even have to have attended the event for it to work.

A LOVING COMMUNITY

Resources and Methods

There is a wide selection of adult and child learning resources available.

- Is it time to look at something different because the material needs new life breathed in to it?
- Have there been so many new initiatives it's time for some continuity?
- Is it important to keep a critical eye on all materials because as the needs of the community change so the methods and materials to teach must be flexible?
- Has our church community changed a lot in the last two years and have we taken note of that in our learning?
- If our community has not changed in composition – what does this say about how people grow in their faith within our church?
- What is the best medium for learning or is a mixture best?
- What approaches to learning best suit your building and people? Can you adapt your building to facilitate learning?

Children's Learning

- Have you got enough people or is the burden on the few? Is it easy to join the team of leaders?
- Do the resources or material give confidence to new volunteers?
- Could you teach in teams so the adults do not become isolated in a world of children's learning and divorced from adult company?

- With the immense variety of children's activities on offer, how can the church captivate imaginations and excite commitment?
- How are effective connections made between the children and the adult members of the church?
- Are there opportunities for the children to lead the adults in worship; as distinct to children performing for adults?
- Have you got people outside your church community who can look astutely and guide wisely and give creative input?

What parts of our learning are appropriate for all ages? What do we do well for different age groups? Could we experiment with times together or apart for eg learning new songs? Or a young people's post confirmation cell group? Or a family teaching morning on a combined theme instead of morning service?

Those who Can

Who have you got who can teach?

- How do you assess someone's potential to teach and move them forward in this work?
- Have you a team that can preach or teach so you cover different approaches and do you use them?
- What training is available in your church or the wider church for teachers or preachers?
- For those in that role for a long while is there training or input available periodically?
- Do those who teach have regular support and feedback that will encourage them?

MARRIAGE ZONE

Questions to apply today's material to marriage

1. How can we 'love God' together?
2. Are the elements of 'loving' as described on Page 56 to be found in our relationships? Are we growing in love?
3. How does major change affect marriage – empty nest, relocation, changing church, etc?
4. How do you communicate love – and how do you most respond to love communicated to you?
5. How can we keep our sexual relationships alive and healthy?

NOTES

Daily Menu

A loyal community

It is an absolute necessity for Christians to clearly know what they believe. Christ is jealous for the truth – and doctrine (believed and lived) is therefore very important. He who is 'the Truth' is calling for a church that is a community of the truth. Loyalty to God and to his truth are important, and will be rewarded by the God who will judge all things in eternity. The Zones will focus on the call to loyalty, and Evening Celebrations will look at how Jesus worked out his loyalties as an adolescent.

Bible passages

Zone outline

Church audit

Evening Celebration

Luke 2:39–52, Jesus the adolescent.
Jesus shows loyalty to God and his family, in that order.

BIBLE PASSAGES

REVELATION

2:12–17 Pergamum

¹²"To the angel of the church in Pergamum write:

These are the words of him who has the sharp, double-edged sword. ¹³I know where you live—where Satan has his throne. Yet you remain true to my name. You did not renounce your faith in me, even in the days of Antipas, my faithful witness, who was put to death in your city—where Satan lives.

¹⁴Nevertheless, I have a few things against you: You have people there who hold to the teaching of Balaam, who taught Balak to entice the Israelites to sin by eating food sacrificed to idols and by committing sexual immorality. ¹⁵Likewise you also have those who hold to the teaching of the Nicolaitans. ¹⁶Repent therefore! Otherwise, I will soon come to you and will fight against them with the sword of my mouth.

¹⁷He who has an ear, let him hear what the Spirit says to the churches. To him who overcomes, I will give some of the hidden manna. I will also give him a white stone with a new name written on it, known only to him who receives it.

2:18–29 Thyatira

¹⁸"To the angel of the church in Thyatira write:

These are the words of the Son of God, whose eyes are like blazing fire and whose feet are like burnished bronze. ¹⁹I know your deeds, your love and faith, your service and perseverance, and that you are now doing more than you did at first.

²⁰Nevertheless, I have this against you: You tolerate that woman Jezebel, who calls herself a prophetess. By her teaching she misleads my servants into sexual immorality and the eating of food sacrificed to idols. ²¹I have given her time to repent of her immorality, but she is unwilling. ²²So I will cast her on a bed of suffering, and I will make those who commit adultery with her suffer intensely, unless they repent of her ways. ²³I will strike her children dead. Then all the churches will know that I am he who searches hearts and minds, and I will repay each of you according to your deeds. ²⁴Now I say to the rest of you in Thyatira, to you who do not hold to her teaching and have not learned Satan's so-called deep secrets (I will not impose any other burden on you): ²⁵Only hold on to what you have until I come.

²⁶To him who overcomes and does my will to the end, I will give authority over the nations—²⁷

    'He will rule them with an iron sceptre;
    he will dash them to pieces like pottery'—

just as I have received authority from my Father. ²⁸I will also give him the morning star. ²⁹He who has an ear, let him hear what the Spirit says to the churches.

NOTES

Journeying with Jesus

You've got Mail

Jesus writes to his church

Aims of this session:

■ Show that truth and theology really matter; there are areas that are fundamental non-negotiables of faith, together with other issues that must remain negotiable.

■ Demonstrate that genuine faith leads to genuine ethical excellence.

■ Show the church as a community of voluntary, redemptive discipline – because of our loyalty to God and our faithfulness to one another.

■ Demonstrate the need for us to be loyal in the exercise of the prophetic, which will require weighing and testing.

■ See that loyalty to Christ should involve extreme reactions to excesses; examples of the prophetic and the leadership of women in the church are illustrations here.

THE CHURCH – A LOYAL COMMUNITY

Two cities tempted by compromise

Pergamum

If Ephesus was like the bustling city of London, then Pergamum (known today as Bergama) had the feel of an old, academic city like Oxford or Cambridge. Proud of its long history, Pergamum was a seat of learning with a fabulous library that held over 200,000 books (every one of them handwritten), a busy medical school and a love of writing – in fact the word *parchment* is derived from the name of the city. A writer of the time described Pergamum as being "like a royal city; the home of authority." Pergamum was the city where the Roman proconsul lived and sat in court session. It had an estimated population of 120,000, and boasted a 3,500 seat theatre.

But beneath the scholarly exterior, Christ saw something very sinister. One Christian had already been publicly executed there.

Christ looked past the academic respectabilities and to "the throne of Satan" established in the place. Why is this phrase used?

Pergamum was certainly rife with occult centres. Not only was there a temple dedicated to the emperor, there were also a wide range of idol worship options available. Zeus, Athena, Dionysus, Demeter, and Hera were honoured – and the city was particularly famous as headquarters for the worship of Asklepios, 'the saviour god' renowned for healing. The serpent was the symbol of the Asklepios cult, which Christians associated with Satan.

The altar to Zeus was very prominent; it stood on a ledge jutting out from a hillside 800 feet above the city; the altar itself was 90 feet square and 20 feet high. Smoke from countless sacrifices would rise all through the day, dominating the skyline. No one could live in Pergamum and not see it.

But most commentators see the strong commitment to emperor worship as the reason for Christ's use of the phrase 'the throne of Satan.'

Pergamum was actually the city with the longest tradition of

A LOYAL COMMUNITY

PERGAMUM: SEAT OF LEARNING

Pergamum was a capital; and such a city has an air and atmosphere all its own. In 133BC its dying king had willed it into the possession of the Roman Empire. Pergamum had become part of the Roman Empire, not by unwilling conquest and compulsion, but by spontaneous choice. The Romans made her the capital of the Province of Asia, and that honour she retained down to AD130. When John wrote his letter Pergamum had been a capital for more than three hundred years.

Pergamum could never attain the commercial eminence and the commanding trade position of Ephesus or Smyrna; its position forbade that. But it was far superior to them in historical greatness. Pergamum was historically the greatest city in Asia Minor – and had all the pride of centuries of greatness behind her.

So close was the connection of Pergamum with literary activity that the word *parchment* is derived from the name Pergamum.

ANTIPAS

Very little is known about this faithful follower of Christ. Legend has it that he was roasted in a bronze bull at the request of Emperor Domitian.

ECHOES FROM PERGAMUM: THE DOCTOR'S SERPENT

The emblem of Asklepios is the serpent, which was intimately connected with one of the ways in which cures were offered in the Asklepeion. Sufferers were allowed to spend the night in the darkness of the temple. In the temple there were tame snakes.

In the night the sufferer might be touched by one of these tame and harmless snakes as it glided over the ground on which he lay. The touch of the snake was held to be the touch of the god himself, and the touch was held to bring health and healing.

Two serpents, the symbol of Askeplios, drink from a dish on this column at the foot of acropolis hill in Pergamum.

THE THRONE OF SATAN

Why did Christ use such strong language to describe the darkness of the city of Pergamum, saying it was "where Satan has his throne"? Commentators have speculated endlessly. Here are some of the suggested reasons:

▶ The Great Altar of Zeus was so prominent there, dominating the skyline

▶ The Roman proconsul lived and ruled from there. After the period of John's revelation, Christians would be brought for trial to Pergamum

▶ The snake temple of Asklepios was there. The god was known as 'saviour', a designation that would obviously be blasphemous to Christians

▶ Antipas was executed there (the only named martyr of the seven churches) and therefore the city was seen as an epicentre of satanic activity

▶ Pergamum was a centre for Graeco-Roman religion generally; the city was, to quote one writer, 'full of idols'

▶ The geography of the city. Approached from the south, a major hill could be seen that had the appearance of a throne

▶ Most modern commentators take the view that Christ describes Pergamum in this way because of the temple to Augustus and the central position it took in the imperial cult and the demand for emperor worship.

Journeying with Jesus

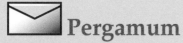 Pergamum

To the angel of the church in Pergamum write:

Rev 2:12

"Pergamum … the Lourdes of the Province of Asia, and the seat of a famous school of medicine."

– R.H. Charles

"The acropolis of Pergamum crowned a steep hill that rose one thousand feet above the plain. Near the summit stood an immense altar to Zeus, erected by Eumenes II to commemorate the victory won by his father over the Gauls; and a short distance from this altar there was an elegant temple of Athena."

– Westminster Dictionary of the Bible

"The imperial cult had its centre in Pergamum."

– R.H. Charles

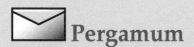 Pergamum

These are the words of him who has the sharp, double-edged sword. I know where you live – where Satan has his throne. Yet you remain true to my name. You did not renounce your faith in me, even in the days of Antipas, my faithful witness, who was put to death in your city – where Satan lives.

Rev 2:12,13

"Pergamum was a dark place. The light of truth filtered only weakly into it. It was steeped in the dense fogs of error."

– John Stott

emperor worship – in 29BC permission was granted to the city fathers for the construction of a temple for the worship of Augustus Caesar. The city loved to be known as the 'temple warden' of Caesar worship. As a result of this, Christian believers there knew very strong opposition. There had been a blatant, overt challenge to them to back off from their loyalty to Christ, during a season that he describes as 'the days of Antipas.' Jesus commends them for their loyalty during that time of testing.

But now they faced more subtle challenges … this time with false teachers. The Christian family at Pergamum that had done so well when confronted with outright opposition was now losing its grip on the truth, allowing erroneous doctrine to be openly spread by false teachers. These doctrines are described as the teaching of Balaam (Rev 2:14) and the teaching of the Nicolaitans (v15).

In summary, the believers at Pergamum were being:
- drawn into sacrifices to idols by eating sacrificial meat (v14)
- drawn into sexual immorality as a result (v14)

Christ calls them to repent and be loyal to the truth (v16). Encouragement is given to those who will overcome (v17) but he threatens to come and fight against the false teachers (v16).

Thyatira

Thirty-five miles down the road in the market city of Thyatira, the church had been doing well – they were commended for their work, their love and faith, their perseverance – and maturing in faith. Unlike the Ephesians, who had fallen from a former height (Rev 2:5), they were doing more than they did at first. Lydia (Acts 16:4) came from this area. Some have suggested that the church here was planted from Ephesus. It was probably quite small.

But here the attack of Satan rages too. The objective was the same – to bring the church into compromise – but the strategy was more subtle. In Pergamum, the believers' lives had been at stake, followed by the introduction of a virus of false teaching. In Thyatira, a thriving trade centre, their livelihoods were under threat if they refused to compromise – and the same virus of false doctrine was being used to compound their sense of confusion.

The great altar of Zeus above the city of Pergamum. This may have been the seat referred to in Rev 2:12 as Satan's throne.

ERROR AT PERGAMUM

Balaam was a pagan prophet hired by Balak, the king of Moab, to pronounce a curse upon the invading Israelites. God caused Balaam to issue a blessing on them instead (Num 22:5–24:25). Balaam subsequently devised a plan in continued disobedience to God whereby some of the Moabite women should entice the Israelite men to "defect from the Lord" (31:16) by fornicating with them and joining with them in the worship of their pagan gods (25:1–3). This plan was successful and God punished the Israelites for their idolatrous involvement. God also commanded Moses to execute the leaders of the people in order that the plague that had broken out upon Israel should go away, but Moses did not immediately obey. Instead he exhorted the leaders to slay those who had actually committed the sins of immorality and idolatry, and even this was not apparently carried out fully. But when Israel did finally discipline itself, the plague was lifted (see Num 25:4–9). Balaam became proverbial for the false teacher who for money influences believers to enter into relationships of compromising unfaithfulness, is warned by God to stop, and is finally punished for continuing to disobey (Num 22:7; Deut 23:4; Neh 13:2; 2 Pet 2:14–16; Jude 5–12).

– *Adapted from* The New International Greek Testament Commentary: The Book of Revelation, *G.K. Beale*

John takes an excursion into Jewish tradition to explain the Nicolaitans' teaching further. After Balak, the king of Moab, had tried without success to persuade Balaam to curse the Israelites during their journey from Egypt (Num 22–24), the Israelite men began to have intercourse with Moabite women, to eat their sacrificed animals and to worship their gods (Num 25:1–3). Jewish tradition (with help from Num 31:16) explained that it was on Balaam's advice that Barak sent Moabite women to seduce the men of Israel into this abandonment of moral and religious purity. So Balaam is remembered in Jewish thought as the originator of religious syncretism – that is, the compromising of one's own faith by mixing it with ideas and practices from other faiths.

Now the Nicolaitans are leading God's people in the same direction. The apostolic decree issued by the Council of Jerusalem in AD49 had forbidden sexual immorality and the eating of food sacrificed to idols (Acts 15:20). In Gentile cities most meat sold in the markets was surplus from pagan temples, where it had been killed for sacrifice to the gods. And meat eating was a main attraction at the special dinners often held at these temples by the trade guilds, which were a common feature of city life. There were guilds of silversmiths, singers, bakers, potters and numerous other crafts.

Paul had reckoned that Christians could eat meat bought in the market, since association with idols who don't really exist anyway could not contaminate it. But they should not eat meals in the temples because that would involve them in worship of false gods (1 Cor 8–10). But the Nicolaitans were not impressed by such views. Sexual immorality too presented no problem to them. Indeed, they vigorously defended it in the name of Christian freedom.

– *Stephen Travis*

Journeying with Jesus

You've got Mail

Jesus writes to his church

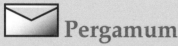 Pergamum

Nevertheless, I have a few things against you: You have people there who hold to the teaching of Balaam, who taught Balak to entice the Israelites to sin by eating food sacrificed to idols and by committing sexual immorality. Likewise you also have those who hold to the teaching of the Nicolaitans.

Rev 2:14

 Thyatira

To the angel of the church in Thyatira write:

These are the words of the Son of God, whose eyes are like blazing fire and whose feet are like burnished bronze. I know your deeds, your love and faith, your service and perseverance, and that you are now doing more than you did at first.

Rev 2:18

www.
http//web link

www.akhisar.com/english

Site of modern day Thyatira.

84

virus warning 🕷️ **ENEMY STRATEGY**
We must be aware that the enemy has more than one strategy in his onslaught against the church. His objectives remain the same, but his strategies will vary according to the strengths and weaknesses of the church.

Apparently anyone who wanted to do business in the city of Thyatira was required to be a member of a trade guild. There were numerous guilds, for bakers and bronze workers, tailors and shoemakers, weavers and tanners, and dyers and potters. These guilds were far more than industrial unions – at their heart were strange ceremonies and feasts that included the worship of pagan deities, and immoral celebrations. All of this put the followers of Jesus in a dilemma:

- ☒ Surely, it could be reasoned, the trade guilds were not all bad. They honoured good citizenship by erecting statues of eminent citizens. They provided occasional dinners to feed the poor of the town.
- ☒ But could a Christian participate in a trade guild with a clear conscience? Would membership of the guilds lead to compromise?
- ☒ If they chose to opt out, how would they trade – and therefore provide for their families?
- ☒ What kind of social rejection would result of them choosing to opt out?
- ☒ Weren't they called to be salt and light in the trade guilds?
- ☒ Some prophetic voices in the church – and the voice of one influential woman in particular – were urging them to go ahead and get involved.

Pergamum and Thyatira: faithfulness required

Be it with brute force and physical threat, or softly softly with intimidation, the objective was the same: to cause the followers of Jesus to waver in their loyalty and compromise their beliefs. Faithfulness and loyalty are at the heart of Christ's call to these two churches.

- ☒ The church at Pergamum is commended for staying true to his name (Rev 2:13)
- ☒ Antipas was Christ's faithful witness (v13)
- ☒ False teachers at Pergamum are having the effect of enticing God's people to sin (v14)
- ☒ The Thyatiran believers have persevered (v19)
- ☒ The Thyatirans that embrace false prophecy are adulterous (v22)

THYATIRA, BUSY MARKET PLACE

Thyatira was not a great religious centre, but it certainly was a great commercial centre. The roads passing through its valley brought the trade of half the world to its doors. In particular, Thyatira was a great centre of the wool trade and of the dyeing industry. It was from Thyatira that Lydia, the seller of purple, came (Acts 16:14). Purple dye was extremely expensive. It came from the little shellfish called the murex. From the throat of this tiny animal one drop of purple dye could be extracted. The elder Pliny tells us that this purple dye was so expensive that one pound of it could not be bought for one thousand denarii, that is, for about seventy thousand dollars. Lydia must have been a merchant princess, a woman of wealth, dealing in one of the most costly substances in the ancient world. Thyatira, then, was a place of great commercial prosperity and wealth.

– William Barclay

TRADE GUILDS

The guilds played a major part in the life of the city, erecting city gates (the tailors guild) as well as colonnades and workmen's houses. Sporting heroes were also commemorated by the guilds; it is clear that the guilds played a strong part of the culture of citizenship.

Two notable features of these guilds are:
- their religious basis. The god Apollo Terminus was evidently conceived inter alia as patron of the guilds, and their feasts were essentially religious occasions that took place in the temple
- their apparent localization. Perhaps the old city was laid out in guild formation. This is parallelled in the layout of the modern town, where the central bazaar is divided by narrow streets into a series of blocks, groups of which are occupied by a single trade. Conspicuous among them are vendors of dyed fabrics and bronzesmiths, who make their goods on the premises.

Journeying with Jesus

You've got Mail

Jesus writes to his church

✉ Thyatira

Nevertheless, I have this against you: You tolerate that woman Jezebel, who calls herself a prophetess. By her teaching she misleads my servants into sexual immorality and the eating of food sacrificed to idols.

Rev 2:20

"It is clear that Thyatira contained more trade guilds than any other town of her size in Asia; and it would seem that the danger which threatened the church at Thyatira was the direct result of the powerful existence of these trade guilds."

– William Barclay

✉ The call to the Thyatirans is to steadfast faithfulness – "Hold on to what you have until I come" (v25) and do God's will "to the end" (v26).

It's been said, "We're not called to be successful, but we're called to be faithful." Some disagree, arguing that faithfulness will lead to success. What do you think?

We've got mail

Perhaps the tale of these two cities seems a long way from where we live, but look again. In a multi-faith culture of relativism and pluralism, the temptation to compromise is very much ours. We too are called to loyalty and faithfulness to Christ. We've got mail again.

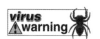

"In Britain in 2002, the only intolerable attitudes that people are dogmatic about are intolerance and dogmatism." Do you agree? Can you think of examples in your own experience?

1. Faithful in doctrine

virus ⚠ warning 🕷 **"TRUTH DOESN'T MATTER"**
Warning: This statement is highly dangerous.

Sometimes, in a real enthusiasm for Christian unity, the suggestion can arise that doctrinal purity is not important.
- ✉ "Love is everything"
- ✉ "Theology doesn't matter – it's unity that counts"
- ✉ "Let's drown our doctrinal differences in Christian love."

The implication is that it doesn't matter what we believe, as long as we are together.

virus ⚠ warning 🕷 **"TRUTH IS EVERYTHING"**
Warning: This statement is highly dangerous.

Some tend to the other extreme, where truth is everything:
- ✉ "We can't have fellowship with any church that believes different doctrine from ours"

PORTRAITS OF FAITHFULNESS

The Epistle to Diognetus, written by an anonymous author around 25 years after Revelation, was discovered in the 16th century. The epistle contrasts the stupidity of idol worship with the beauty of Christian conduct and community. Here is a paraphrased excerpt:

"It's not possible to tell a Christian from an unbeliever by where he lives, what he wears or the way he dresses. There are no Christian towns, there is no Christian language. They eat, sleep and drink in exactly the same way as everyone else. Christians aren't particularly clever or ingenious and they haven't mastered some complicated formula, like the followers of other religions. But while it's true that they live in cities next door to other people and follow the same pattern of ordinary daily life as they do, in fact they possess a unique citizenship of their own. They are, of course, faithful and loyal citizens of their own lands, but they feel visitors there. In a strange paradox, every foreign country is their homeland, and their homeland is a foreign country to them.

"Destiny has determined that they should live here on earth in the flesh, but they do not live for the flesh. Their days are passed on earth, but their real citizenship is in heaven. They obey the laws of the powers that be, but in their own lives they live by a higher law. They show love to everyone – and everyone seems to persecute them. They are constantly misunderstood and misrepresented; yet through their suffering they find life. They are poor, but make many rich. They lack many things, yet have everything that matters in abundance. In their dishonour they are made glorious, in being slandered they are eternally vindicated. They repay insults with blessings and abuse with courtesy."

– From After the Gospels – Readings from great Christians of the early church, *David Winter*

IT'S FOR US AGAIN

- We live in a culture where tolerance is a prized virtue – perhaps the only thing that our culture won't tolerate is intolerance! Postmodernism means that many ideas can sit alongside each other – it is only when one tries to designate a belief as the absolute truth that the trouble begins; and the Christian follows the Christ who affirms: "I am the way and the truth and the life" (John 14:6)
- We want to avoid arrogance and dogmatism – but that can mean we begin tolerating what we should not, in the name of reason and compassion
- We live in a multi-faith culture, and need to treat other faiths with dignity and respect – and indeed be willing to campaign for religious liberty for all faiths, not just our own. But in engaging in respectful dialogue with other faiths, we must be faithful to the uniqueness of Christ and all of his claims
- The church in the third millennium is seeking cultural relevance – we want to communicate with clarity to our culture, and we need to be willing to adapt and change to meet its needs. But cultural *relevance* does not mean cultural *conformity*. When the church refuses to challenge the culture, it becomes shaped by it. The pathway between fundamentalist intolerance and liberal tolerance is narrow
- Have you ever heard Christians complain that things are getting worse and worse when they consider the moral and spiritual landscape of the area they live in? Notice that we can tend to think the city, town, village or country where we live is 'the hardest place' when it comes to receptivity to the gospel? The Christians in Pergamum must have felt like that; Christ knew what a hard, tough place they lived in
- We must be grateful for the gift of prophecy being manifested in the church; but this demands that we treat the prophetic with maturity and discernment.

Journeying with Jesus

You've got MaiL

Jesus writes to his church

"Love becomes sentimental if it is not strengthened by truth, and truth becomes hard if it is not softened by love. We need to preserve the balance of the Bible, which tells us to hold the truth in love, to love others in the truth, and to grow not only in love but discernment (Eph 4:15, 3 John 1, Phil 1:9)."

– *John Stott*

- ⊠ "They're compromisers"
- ⊠ "Never mind unity – we need to stay apart from the other churches to stay doctrinally pure."

Press to reply

Love that has no concern for truth; or a hard-line obsession with doctrinal orthodoxy – do you tend more to one direction than the other?

There is a balanced pathway we must walk if we are to be faithful and loyal to Christ and to the truth of the gospel. Truth is absolutely vital and important.

- ⊠ Christ is concerned for truth – He will fight and judge the false teachers of Pergamum and Thyatira (Rev 2:16,22)
- ⊠ He calls himself 'the truth' (John 14:6) and says he came to 'testify to the truth' (John 18:37)
- ⊠ He says the truth sets us free (John 8:32)
- ⊠ Paul continually stood his ground on behalf of the truth of the gospel (Gal 2:14).

But what is truth? What are the essentials about which we cannot negotiate, and what are the issues where there can be a variety of approaches without unity being compromised?

The truth about Christ

John Stott suggests two areas where we must diligently hold fast to the truth. The first non-negotiable is the truth about Christ.

Some of the Christians at Pergamum had been commanded to declare that Caesar was lord – but refused to negotiate on that core truth.

"You remained true to my name. You did not renounce your faith in me" (Rev 2:13).

To deny the divinity of Christ is nothing less than functioning in the spirit of antichrist (1 John 2:22, 4:2, 2 John 7–11). Paul emphatically declares that a gospel that denies Christ's saving grace is anathema (Gal 1:6–9).

Statue of one of Rome's elite Praetorian Guard.

STRAINING OUT GNATS AND SWALLOWING CAMELS

In our efforts to guard truth we sometimes:

- Minimize the essential
- Magnify the peripheral
- Concede on non-negotiables
- Insist on trivialities
- End up in an unloving attitude – and to love God and hate our brother or sister is impossible (1 John 4:20)
- Don't speak the truth in love (Eph 4:15) – and when we don't speak in love, we fail to speak the truth
- Fail to love the truth: to be saved one must love the truth (2 Thess 2:10, 13)
- Fail to know the truth: to be saved is to come to a knowledge of the truth (1 Tim 2:4)

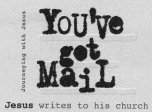

2. Faithful in ethics and integrity
The truth about holiness

The second non-negotiable, according to Stott, is the truth about holiness. Specific details of holy living are a matter of conscience and debate – we must make room for differences of opinion about these matters.

We must concede that behavioural norms are moulded by a variety of influences, including:

- Interpretation of scripture, which in turn is shaped by:
  - Culture
  - History and tradition
  - Leadership style (some churches have a more definite line on certain issues)
  - the 'flavour' of church to which we belong.

virus ⚠warning 🕷 **EXTRA-BIBLICAL RULEBOOK**
Be highly suspect of a Christianity built around extra-biblical rules and regulations with no logical foundation that are the product of tradition ('that's the way we live in our church') or overbearing leadership ('our leader/minister says so, so it must be right').

Genuine belief affects behaviour: this is beyond doubt. To suggest that to follow Christ makes no difference to our integrity or morality is to propagate blatant error (1 John 2:4, 1 Cor 5:11). In both churches there were seducing influences leading believers away from authentic holiness.

- Balaam, taught Balak to entice the Israelites to sin (Rev 2:14)
- She misleads my people into sexual immorality (v20)

virus ⚠warning 🕷 **ORTHODOXY IS NOT ENOUGH**
In New Testament terms, theological orthodoxy is vital but not enough. Truth is expressed in lifestyle as well as belief system. And the reverse of this is true – bad doctrine leads to bad behaviour.

Turn around

The churches of Pergamum and Thyatira included members who had crossed the line into behaviour that was unacceptable to Christ. They were:

- Called to repent (Rev 2:16)

"You are a king, then!" said Pilate.
Jesus answered, "You are right in saying I am a king. In fact, for this reason I was born, and for this I came into the world, to testify to the truth. Everyone on the side of truth listens to me."
"What is truth?" Pilate asked.
– John 18:37–38

ROOM FOR OPINIONS

For example, some issues of conduct about which Christians widely disagree are:

▶ **Pacifism** – some believe that violence is always wrong and can never be justified. Others accept what is often called the 'doctrine of the just war'

▶ **Divorce and remarriage** – some hold the view that if you are divorced then it is wrong to remarry. Others believe this is a valid option for a Christian

▶ **Alcohol consumption** – although all would agree that excess or drunkenness is wrong

▶ **Smoking** – in some European countries the elders get together to smoke a cigar or cigarette after the morning service

▶ **Purchasing on Sundays** – and approaches to keeping Sunday special

▶ **Approaches to entertainment** – cinema, theatre, etc.

DECISIONS, DECISIONS

The powerful trade guilds in the city of Thyatira would have made it very difficult for any Christian to earn a living without belonging to a guild. But membership involved attendance at guild banquets, and this in turn meant eating meat which had first been sacrificed to an idol. What was the Christian to do? If he did not conform he was out of a job. Jezebel apparently reasoned that an idol was of no consequence (cf. 1 Cor 8:4) and advised Christians to eat such meals. That these meals all too readily degenerated into sexual looseness made matters worse. But we can understand that some Christians would welcome a heresy of this kind. It enabled them to maintain a Christian profession while countenancing and even engaging in immoral heathen revels. That Jezebel was a prophetess gave their course some standing.

We should not minimize the importance of the question at issue, nor the difficulty some first-century Christians must have had in seeing the right course. Nor should we dismiss the problem as only of academic interest since it does not concern us. Every generation of Christians must face the question, 'How far should I accept and adopt contemporary standards and practices?'

On the one hand, Christians must not deny the faith. On the other, they must not deny their membership of society. The cause of Christ is not served if Christians appear as a group of old-fashioned people always trying to retreat from the real world. Christians live in the same world as their neighbours and face the same problems. They must find Christian solutions. The prophetess and her followers had been so ready to conform to the practices of their heathen neighbours that they had lost sight of the essential Christian position. They had exalted expediency over principle. Had Christianity taken this way it must surely have become just another of the eastern cults that had their little day and perished. The risen Lord points to the very essence of Christian living when he urges high standards of moral conduct.

– Leon Morris

> ✉ Threatened with severe judgement (v22)
> ✉ About to be made an example for all the churches (v23)
> ✉ About to discover Christ's justice and retribution (v23)
> ✉ Called to discover that those who follow Jesus don't behave in a particular way just because everyone's doing it.

Press to reply

Have you tried to divide your life into compartments – and realized there are elements of your lifestyle that are wholly incompatible with following Christ?

Discipline: You tolerate that woman…

The church at Thyatira had tolerated false teaching that led to immorality. Corporately, they had abdicated their responsibility to maintain biblical standards of purity in the church. The Thyatirans mirrored a problem that had developed in Corinth, where an 'immoral brother' was following an impure lifestyle (sleeping with his stepmother) without challenge or rebuke (1 Cor 5:1). Paul encouraged the Corinthians to exercise firm but loving discipline, in order that the church might not be bought into disrepute (1 Cor 5:4–5,13).

Church discipline is vital if we are not to fall into the trap of false toleration. But it is also fraught with difficulty. The situation in Corinth illustrates this. The Corinthians were so eager to correct their error of false tolerance that they became harsh and unforgiving, and Paul had to write again to encourage them to "forgive and comfort him, … reaffirm your love for him" (2 Cor 2:7–8). Church discipline takes place when the church together makes a clear stand over a believer's behaviour, when it is clearly inconsistent with the truth of the gospel. It is a difficult but vital act of loyalty to Christ and to one another. But we must avoid the extremes of easy toleration or harshness.

3. Faithful approach to the prophetic

In Thyatira, a self-styled prophetess was apparently encouraging the church to get fully involved in the guilds. The argument is persuasive – they are not under law any longer, so why not fully immerse themselves in pagan society, even to the extent of exploring 'Satan's so-called deep secrets' (Rev 2:24). This prophetess is known as Jezebel. Christians are now participating in occult worship, and giving themselves to blatant sexual immorality. Remember the situation down the road at Pergamum – here too, in Thyatira, believers

---

"We must preserve unity in essentials, liberty in non-essentials and charity in all things."

– Rupert Meldenius

"It is God's will that you should be sanctified: that you should avoid sexual immorality; that each of you should learn to control his own body in a way that is holy and honourable, not in passionate lust like the heathen, who do not know God."

– 1 Thessalonians 4:3–5

A LOYAL COMMUNITY

EVERYONE'S DOING IT

The prevalence of sexual immorality in first-century pagan society makes it entirely possible that some Christians at Pergamum were still participating in the holiday festivities and saw no wrong in indulging in the harmless table in the temples and the sexual excitement everyone else was enjoying (cf. 1 John 5:21). Will Durant made the following observation on the pagan festivities:

"At the centre and summit of each Greek city was the shrine of the city god; participation in the worship of the god was the sign, the privilege, and the requisite of citizenship. In the spring, the Greek cities celebrated the *Athesterion*, or feast of powers, a three-day festival to Dionysus [a chief deity at Pergamum] in which wine flowed freely and everybody was more or less drunk. At the end of March came the great *Dionysia*, a widely observed series of processions and plays accompanied by general revelry. At the beginning of April various cities in Greece celebrated Aphrodite's great festival, the *Aphrodisia*; and on that occasion, for those who cared to take part, sexual freedom was the order of the day."

– *Adapted from* The Story of Civilisation, Vol. 2, Life of Greece, *Simon and Schuster*

DO NOT BE DECEIVED

We do well to remember that deception is married to sin; the believers at Pergamum were enticed (as were the Israelites of old) and the Thyatirans misled. Whenever popularity becomes more important than conviction, or we accept the values of those around us without question, we begin to step over the line into sin and that invokes Christ's anger. When we try to compartmentalize our lives, living one set of beliefs on Sunday and another in Monday, we move towards that line. When we try to domesticate Jesus and make him a source of encouragement, but never a source of challenge and rebuke, we move into dangerous territory. But this should not lead us to the other extreme of asceticism: an extreme rigidity or a burdensome religiosity.

CHURCH DISCIPLINE

We should recognise that church discipline:

▶ **Is for the believer.** The church should be a safe haven for sinners to be able to examine the claims of Christ. If discipline is exacted upon anyone who even attends a church, then we end up with only those who meet our standards – thus the church is always looking for a better class of sinner

▶ **Is for the committed believer.** It can only operate where believers are voluntarily submitting themselves to the corporate discipline of a local church

▶ **Should take consideration of the direction of a believer's life.** If a brand new Christian is living in an immoral situation, this requires patient discipleship – not discipline. If a leader or a deacon is found in persistent sin, this will require a different response

▶ **Is an act of faithfulness to one another.** God disciplines those that he loves (Heb 12:6) and because we are concerned for one another's good (Heb 12:10) we should act lovingly to bring restoration to one another's lives

▶ **May be abused.** Where a leadership has a dictatorial style, or there is a legalistic approach to ethics in a local church, church discipline can be misused by a manipulative or controlling leadership, as in the case of Diotrephes (3 John 1:10)

▶ **Is designed to be redemptive.** Church discipline has restoration as its goal, not punishment (Matt 18:15, Gal 6:1)

▶ **Can only function when there is a recognition that the church is not perfect**, and never will be this side of eternity – hence the teaching of Christ on the wheat and tares (Matt 13:24–30, 36–43)

▶ **Should avoid an obsession with sexual sin** while ignoring other issues such as idolatry, jealousy, greed and selfish ambition (Gal 5:19–21, Eph 5:5–6)

▶ **Is a slow process** which will always make room for repentance and restoration (Matt 18:15–17)

▶ **Is designed to culminate in kindness** and generosity to the repentant (Matt 18:10–14)

are being:

- ✉ drawn into sacrifices to idols by eating sacrificial meat
- ✉ drawn into immorality as a result.

virus ⚠**warning** 🕷 **BEWARE DECEPTION**
False prophecy is convincing, otherwise it would have no power of deception.

📖 bo|ok
.link
The Beginner's Guide to The Gift of Prophecy, Jack Deere, Kingsway Publications

Consider the situation in Thyatira.

- ✉ Someone is apparently speaking 'words from the Lord'
- ✉ They argue that we are 'free in Christ'
- ✉ They say that they are following a 'deeper' faith than ours
- ✉ The pathway they advocate will allow us to trade freely
- ✉ The prophetess argues that idols are dead anyway.

Press to reply

Think how you might have felt if you had lived in Thyatira. Wouldn't you be attracted by this message?

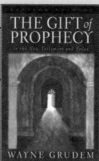

📖 bo|ok
.link
The Gift of Prophecy, Wayne Grudem, Kingsway Publications

Don't demonize women – or prophecy
Women in ministry and leadership

There was a problem with a female 'charismatic' in Thyatira – which does not mean we should react negatively to the idea of women in ministry, or against the gifts of the Holy Spirit. As we will see, that is exactly what the early church did. But women's ministry was very common in the early church.

However, the negative examples of the so-called Jezebel, together with two women (Priscilla and Maximilla) who had left their husbands and travelled around prophesying, brought women's ministry into disrepute. (Priscilla and Maximilla were well known for their love of make up and money.)

The combination of weird prophecies and materialistic lifestyles brought notoriety upon both women leaders. By the time of the third century, it was written into the *Didascalia* (a work on church organization) that women could be deacons but were excluded from preaching.

Pergamum

Repent therefore! Otherwise, I will soon come to you and will fight against them with the sword of my mouth.

Rev 2:16

The gift of prophecy

Scripture clearly states that the gift of prophecy, as with all of the gifts of God, is vital and helpful for the edification and building up

A LOYAL COMMUNITY

THE POWER OF PROPHECY

Ignatius (c.35–c.110) was probably the third bishop of Antioch.

Not a great deal is known about him until his arrest in one of the periodic Roman sweeps against dissident groups, including Christians. With several others, he was shipped to Rome to be fed to wild beasts in the arena. The journey there was a long one, under the supervision of ten armed guards, and during various stops Ignatius took the opportunity to meet the leaders of local churches and deliver to each of them a pastoral letter. These letters form the substance of the heritage he has left to us. During the journey, Ignatius visited Laodicea, Philadelphia, Sardis and Smyrna, where representatives of the churches at Tralles, Magnesia and Ephesus had come to meet him and salute the martyr-delegate. To each of these churches, and to the visiting leaders, he handed over a letter. Here, paraphrased into modern English, are some of his instructions about prophecy.

"Now of course I am not infallible! Like everyone else, I can be mistaken. But the Holy Spirit cannot be mistaken, nor can he be deceived, because he is the Spirit of God, and God is infallible.

"Let me give you an example. When I visited the church at Philadelphia there was a faction there, a group who were undermining the church's leadership and constantly opposing their decisions. Now God is my witness that I knew nothing about this at all. No one had told me of it and no rumour of it had reached my ears.

"So when I stood up to prophesy, and shouted in a loud voice, 'Give more respect to your bishop, your elders and your deacons!', it was the Holy Spirit who was speaking in me. Although I know some people think I had been told in advance of the divisions at Philadelphia, and spoke from prior knowledge, the absolute truth is that this was the voice of God alone.

"So, remember that, and remember and obey the other things I said as well: 'Keep your bodies as temples of God. Love unity. Shun divisions. Follow Jesus Christ, as he followed his Father.'"

WOMEN IN LEADERSHIP

The issue of women and their role in church leadership is one where Christians take widely differing views. As people who trust the Bible's authority, we need to listen carefully to each other and respect one another's conclusions.

▶ Some see the instructions issued in Paul's letters – to Timothy and the church in Corinth for example – as clearly excluding women from certain roles. See 1 Tim 2:8–3:13 and 1 Cor 14:33–30. Others observe that Jesus chose only men as his apostles.

▶ Those taking a different view point out that this simply reflected the culture of the day. They point to Jesus' radically inclusive approach to women and a wider Scriptural view, including Paul's statement that "There is neither Jew nor Greek, slave nor free, male nor female, for you are all one in Christ Jesus" (Gal 3:26–29).

EXAMPLES OF WOMEN IN LEADERSHIP IN THE EARLY CHURCH

▶ Prior to the errors and excess of Montanism, prophets could be of either sex
▶ The first convert from the Thyatira area was Lydia, who was converted while on a business trip to Philippi (Acts 16:14–15). Believers gathered at her house
▶ Priscilla was involved in leadership at Ephesus and Corinth
▶ Nympha was involved at Colossae (Col 4:15)
▶ The 'unknown lady' was written to by John (2 John)
▶ Jezebel was obviously in a place of influence – and was criticized not for being a woman in leadership, but for her false teaching
▶ Philip's four daughters were highly respectable preachers
▶ Ammia was a highly respected prophet at Philadelphia
▶ The early third century school of instruction led by Origen had women and men in attendance in equal status
▶ Ladies like Herais and Potamiana were graduates of Origen's school and soon after suffered martyrdom for their faith
▶ As late as the fourth century there were outstanding women in the monastic movement, and imperial ladies who got involved in the theological debates of their day.

"In the second century there were quite a few charismatic females of unimpeachable orthodoxy, whose ministry was recognized and affirmed by the mainstream churches."

– Mike Smith

"Prophecy was almost completely dropped in favour of more sober preaching and the exposition of the Scriptures. There are no references to speaking in tongues, and miraculous healings become very rare. Exorcism became ritualized into the pronouncement and prayers over those being baptized. It was almost as if the shutter had come down. The effect of Montanism had been to make everyone very cautious of any charismatic signs. ... in the Washington Codex of the gospels (also written in the fourth century) the 'Long Ending' of Mark's Gospel is altered so as to cut out all mention of 'signs following'."

– Mike Smith

of the body of Christ. Prophecy can be predictive (proclaiming the future) and/or exhortative (proclaiming the truth).

- The Holy Spirit is the author of the gift (Acts 2:17, 2 Pet 1:21)
- Believers are exhorted to desire to prophesy (1 Cor 14:1,5,39)
- The gift is for the good of the church (1 Cor 14:6)
- Prophecy is a sign for believers (1 Cor 14:22)

But the gift of prophecy can be misused, used falsely, and exercised without maturity causing the church to become unsettled (2 Thess 2:2), put too much faith in the prophetic (1 Cor 13:9), and get into chaos and disorder (1 Cor 14:31–33).

The key, ongoing weakness in Thyatira was lack of discernment and unwillingness to weigh or judge the so-called prophetic statements given by Jezebel (1 Cor 14:29, 1 Thess 5:21, 1 John 4:21). The same can be true for us today.

Prophecy:

- Must always honour Christ (John 16:14, 1 Cor 12:3)
- Must always honour and be consistent with the teaching of Christ and his apostles (Matt 7:20–23, 1 John 4:6)
- Must build up the church (1 Cor 14:3–4)
- Must be delivered in love (1 Cor 13)
- Must be confirmed and received by the wider church congregation (1 Cor 14:29)

Some Christians hold the view that gifts of the Spirit such as prophecy died out at the end of the apostolic period. Such a view is called 'cessationist' as the gifts ceased to operate. Other Christians believe the prophetic is experienced through biblical preaching.

 BEHIND CLOSED DOORS

Because of the need for prophecy to be judged, we should be especially cautious about personalized prophecies given to one individual. One guideline might be that prophecies of this type are always shared with a wider group for their weighing, so that prophecy may be personal but never private. Private prophecy is an open door for confusion and even manipulation.

The early church was used to the supernatural and the prophetic. Irenaeus spoke of miraculous healings, genuine speaking in tongues, predictive prophecies, and even a few cases of dead people being raised. Much was expected in terms of moral excellence and

PROPHECY

Prophets function primarily in the worship of the church (Acts 13:2). They predict (Acts 11:28, 20:23, 27:22–26), announce judgments (Acts 13:11, 28:25–28), act symbolically (Acts 21:10–11), and receive visions (Acts 9:10–11; 2 Cor 12:1). Prophetic insights led to missionary efforts (Acts 13:1–3, 10:10–17, 15:28,32). While teaching and prophecy are different, they also can be related (Acts 13:1–2; Rev 2:20). Some prophets preached lengthy messages (Acts 15:32) and gave exposition to biblical texts (Luke 1:67–79; Eph 3:5; Rom 11:25–36).

The prophets used phrases such as 'the Lord says' or 'the Holy Spirit says' as introductory formulas for prophetic insight into the future (Acts 21:11), or for inspired adaptation of an Old Testament text (Heb 3:7).

New Testament prophecy was limited (1 Cor 13:9); it was to be evaluated by the congregation (1 Cor 14:29; 1 Thess 5:20–21). One may even respond inappropriately to prophecy (Acts 21:12). The supreme test for prophecy is loyalty to Christ (1 Cor 12:3; Rev 19:10). Some Christians have the gift of discernment (1 Cor 12:10). Jesus said prophets could be known by their fruit (Matt 7:15–20). Paul demanded orderly, Christ-honouring, up-building prophecy that submits to apostolic authority (1 Cor 14:26–40). Thus prophecy is not without restraint. Circumstance may even demand that the dress of men and women prophets be stipulated (1 Cor 11:5–7). Prophecy outside of apostolic authority can be safely ignored; thus prophecy is not a threat to Scripture's special authority (1 Cor 14:38–39; 2 Tim 3:16; 2 Pet 1:20–21).

– Holman Bible Dictionary, *Randy Hatchett*

PROPHECY AND PREACHING

Prophesying is in principle a universal Christian activity, so far from expecting to find it confined to the apostolic age, we should not expect to find it absent in any age, and therefore we should be somewhat suspicious of theories that assume that it has been absent for most of the church's life. Though individual prophets both before and after Christ were on occasion inspired to tell the future (Matt 24:15; Acts 11:28; 21:10,11; 1 Peter 1:10–12; Rev 1:3; 22:18), the essence of the prophetic ministry was forthtelling God's present word to his people, and this regularly meant application of revealed truth rather than augmentation of it.

The proper conclusion surely is that, rather than supposing prophecy to be a long-gone first-century charisma now revived and therefore to be dressed up in verbal clothes that will set it apart from all other forms of communication over the past 18 or 19 centuries, we should realise that it has actually been exhibited in every sermon or informal 'message' that has had a heartsearching, 'home-coming' application to its hearers, ever since the church began. Preaching and teaching God's revealed truth with application; such teaching with application is prophecy, always was, and always will be and is no more so among charismatics today than at any time in any other Christian company, past, present, or future.

– Keep in Step with the Spirit, *J.I. Packer, I.V.P.*

You've got Mail

Jesus writes to his church

accountability from prophets. The abuse of prophecy in the early church by Marcus (who apparently required money and sexual favours in return for the privilege of being made a prophetess) and then the errors of the Montanists began to bring prophecy into disrepute. This movement began with a convert called Montanus (from the village of Ardabau) speaking in tongues, but progressed to strange prophecies about the end of the world – the New Jerusalem would appear at small Phrygian villages called Pepuza and Tymion. One Montanist prophet declared that the colour of the soul was sky blue. Then the Montanists began to claim direct authority from the Holy Spirit, saying their prophecies were on the same level as Scripture. Many dying martyrs denounced the Montanists, not wanting to be associated with them.

There were gatherings of leaders to discuss a response to the Montanists, and growing scepticism towards the prophetic developed. Eusebius' Church History mentions little in terms of the miraculous.

- ✉ Second century martyrs went to their deaths with visions and prophecies of encouragement (eg Perpetua of Carthage)
- ✉ Third and fourth century martyrs did not have this experience
- ✉ It was not until the early part of the fifth century that charismatic signs were seen again (for example in the ministries of Martin of Tours, and Germanus of Auxerre).

 MISUSE ≠ DISUSE

Misuse and abuse of the gifts of God should not lead us to disuse and abandonment.

Really good news for the faithful

Good news: Christ knows your address – even if you live in a hard place

The letter to Pergamum is the only mail where Christ says, "I know where you live" (Rev 2:13). He takes pains to let the believers know he is fully aware of their difficult hard location. When you live in a hard place for the Gospel, it can feel that God is distant and uninvolved. On the contrary, he knows fully.

Good news: Christ again is the true ruler

The city of Pergamum had been granted special permission to exact

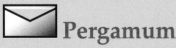 **Pergamum**

He who has an ear, let him hear what the Spirit says to the churches. To him who overcomes, I will give some of the hidden manna. I will also give him a white stone with a new name written on it, known only to him who receives it.

Rev 2:17

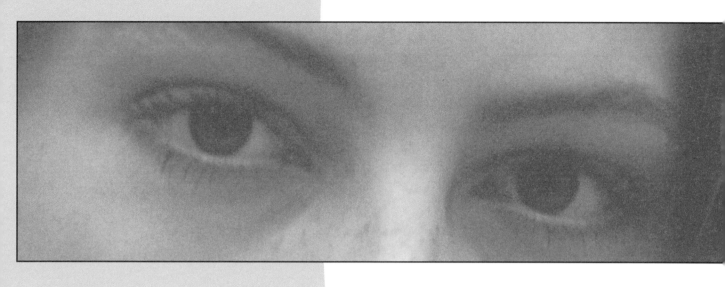

PROPHECY, THE EARLY CHURCH AND JEZEBEL

The genuine gift of prophecy was highly respected in the early church. Along with apostles, teachers and elders, prophets were often elevated to leadership (1 Cor 12:28; Eph 4:11). Women also received the genuine gift of prophecy (Luke 2:36; Acts 21:9; 1 Cor 11:5). Prophets generally brought direct revelation from God in the form of teaching as well as occasional predictions of the future (Acts 11.27). Tests for a true prophet, as for the true apostle (Rev 2:2), were available but often difficult to apply.

This supposedly Christian woman at Thyatira had claimed to be a prophetess, gifted as such by the Holy Spirit. She must have been elevated to prominence in church because of her unusual gifts. A small minority saw through her pious deception (Rev 2:24); the rest either followed her or ignored her views without objecting to her presence in the church. In order to expose her true character, she is labelled 'Jezebel' – the name of the Canaanite wife of Israel's King Arab. Jezebel had not only led Ahab to worship Baal but through Ahab had promulgated her teachings of idolatry throughout all Israel (1 Kings 16:31–33; 2 Kings 9:22).

We must not press the similarity too far, however. As this wicked and deceptive woman in the Old Testament led Israel astray and persecuted the true prophets of God, so this woman at Thyatira was enticing the servants of God to abandon their exclusive loyalty to Christ. Her teaching was no doubt similar to that of the Nicolaitans and Balaamites at Ephesus and Pergamum. While most commentators prefer to see the 'sexual immorality' as spiritual adultery (i.e., idolatry), the possibility of cultic fornication should not be ruled out.

 ## Thyatira

I have given her time to repent of her immorality, but she is unwilling. So I will cast her on a bed of suffering, and I will make those who commit adultery with her suffer intensely, unless they repent of her ways. I will strike her children dead. Then all the churches will know that I am he who searches hearts and minds, and I will repay each of you according to your deeds. Now I say to the rest of you in Thyatira, to you who do not hold to her teaching and have not learned Satan's so-called deep secrets (I will not impose any other burden on you): Only hold on to what you have until I come. To him who overcomes and does my will to the end, I will give authority over the nations – 'He will rule them with an iron sceptre; he will dash them to pieces like pottery' – just as I have received authority from my Father. I will also give him the morning star. He who has an ear, let him hear what the Spirit says to the churches.

Rev2:21–29

capital punishment (*ius gladii*) – the sword was in the hands of the city, courtesy of the almost unlimited authority of the Roman proconsul who lived there. But Christ has "the sword of my mouth" (Rev 2:16, 1:16).

And in Thyatira, they learn of the Christ who has feet "of burnished bronze". The coppersmiths of Thyatira had developed a sophisticated technique enabling them to produce the finest brass. But Christ is revealed as the warrior in the finest armour; the mighty defender of his church.

Likewise, the Thyatirans are encouraged that the real morning star is theirs as they have Christ himself (Rev 2:28). (Balaam prophesied about the morning star in Num 14:27.) For the Thyatirans living in the Roman Empire, this has special significance: the Romans believed that the morning star was Venus, a goddess and the symbol of authority adopted by the Caesars, who claimed to be descended from her. Emperor Domitian was flattered in one poem comparing him to the morning star. Christ is making it clear: Jesus, not Caesar, is really in charge.

Good news: you're on first-name terms with Jesus, and invited to his banquet

The overcomers in the church at Pergamum are promised some of the 'hidden manna' and a 'white stone with a new name written on it'. There was a Jewish tradition that when Messiah came, he would bring with him a sample of the old manna given in the wilderness to those wanderers.

Remember the Balaam reference? Just as ancient Israel, tempted by Balaam, was provided for by God with manna, so the faithful who refused to be tempted by the banqueting tables of Pergamum would be sustained and nourished by Christ.

The white stone may refer to
- ☒ The custom of giving a stone to a man at the end of his trial – white for not guilty and black for guilty. Perhaps this is a tender encouragement about forgiveness
- ☒ White stones were also used as admission tickets at festivals; there is certain admission at Christ's banquet for the loyal and faithful
- ☒ The new name is almost certainly the name of Christ, which

SWORD OF HIS MOUTH

Concerned that his church stand in the truth, and recognizing the source of error, Jesus Christ is resolved that the truth shall triumph. He calls upon the church of Pergamum, which has permitted grievous error to be taught unchecked, both to repent (Rev 2:16) and to gain the victory over falsehood. He then indicates both the way of conquest and its reward.

The way of conquest is by his word. The only weapon able to slay the forces of error is the word of Christ. No wonder, as he dictates this letter to John, he describes himself as he who has the sharp, double-edged sword (v12). In John's vision of the exalted Christ, as described in the first chapter of Revelation, this sharp double-edged sword came from Jesus' mouth (Rev 1:16) because it is a symbol of the word of truth he has spoken. Indeed, he is himself the Word of God (Rev 19:13; compare John 1:1).

The picture of Christ with a sword flashing from his mouth may seem to us peculiar, but is not so strange as it appears for the short Roman sword was tongue-like in shape (Hastings' Dictionary of the Bible). In the prophecy of Isaiah the Servant of Yahweh (prefiguring Christ) says: "He made my mouth like a sharpened sword" (Isa 49:2). The word of God is said by the apostle Paul to be the sword of the Spirit, and in Hebrews he calls it living and active. "Sharper than any double-edged sword, it penetrates even to dividing soul and spirit, joints and marrow; it judges the thoughts and attitudes of the heart" (Heb 4:12). Whether or not we agree with Tertullian (c.160–c.225) and Augustine that the two edges of the sword represent the Old and New Testaments, the Bible has many sword-like qualities. It pricks the conscience, and wounds the pride of sinners. It cuts away our camouflage and pierces our defences. It lays bare our sin and need, and kills all false doctrine by its deft, sharp thrusts.

God's way to overcome error is the proclamation of the gospel of Christ, which is God's power for salvation to everyone who believes. Falsehood will not be suppressed by the gruesome methods of the inquisition, or by the burning of heretics at the stake, or by restrictive legislation. Ideas will not be overcome by force. Only truth can defeat error. The false ideologies of the world can be overthrown only by the superior ideology of Christ. We have no weapon other than this sword. We must use it fearlessly.

One day this same sword will change its function. The message of truth will become the message of judgment. The sword to pierce the conscience will be the sword to destroy the soul. "I will soon come to you and will fight against them with the sword of my mouth" (Rev 2:16; compare Rev 19:15,21). Balaam himself was killed with the sword (Num 31:8; Josh 13:22), and the Balaamites in Pergamum (unless they repent) will suffer the same fate, except that now the sword will be the word of Christ. In other words the very gospel of Christ which saves those who obey it destroys those who disobey it.

If anything is certain about divine judgment in Scripture, it is that God will hold us responsible for our response to that measure of truth which we have known. And from those to whom much is revealed, much will be required. As Jesus said to his contemporaries: "As for the person who hears my words but does not keep them, I do not judge him. For I did not come to judge the world, but to save it. There is a judge for the one who rejects me and does not accept my words; that very word which I spoke will condemn him at the last day" (John 12:47,48). Here is Christ's saving word turned judge, his wholesome sword turned executioner.

– John Stott

is secret because eternity alone will reveal the full nature and rewards that Christ will bestow upon his beloved people.

Good news: one day the ruled will rule

The Thyatirans are promised that one day they will reign with Christ (Rev 2:26–27). One day, the saints of God will judge the world (1 Cor 6:2, see also Matt 25:21,23, Luke 19:17). This does not suggest earthly vengeance, but rather an acknowledgement by some of the enemies of the gospel that the struggling churches really do have the life and truth of Christ.

But to those who will not repent (Rev 2:16,21) in both cities, judgement is coming.

- ✉ Christ will fight them with his sword (v16)
- ✉ Jezebel and her children will suffer (v22)
- ✉ Some will die (v23)
- ✉ All the churches will know that Christ searches hearts and minds, as the God of justice (v23)

RSVP

So how did they respond to their mail?
Pergamum

- ✉ The church there did continue – there were two notable martyrs, Carpus and Papylus, and a woman called Agathonice who "after many noble declarations of their belief found glorious fulfilment" (Eusebius)
- ✉ Eusebius makes only casual reference to Pergamum, perhaps suggesting the work there was not significant
- ✉ Seventy years after the church at Pergamum got mail, one of its strongest members, Attalus, who had always been a pillar and support of the church in his native Pergamum, was martyred. Probably from a well-to-do family, he was a Roman citizen and an enthusiastic believer who moved from Pergamum to live in Lyons. He was tortured in the arena, and later thrown to wild beasts, which did not kill him. In the end he was chained to an iron chair and burned alive. He refused to deny his faith; his burned body was left unburied for six days, and then the ashes were thrown into the River Rhone.
- ✉ Apart from this, there is silence about the Pergamum church in

The Trajanum in Pergamum.

the second and third centuries. Pergamum never became great for Christ.

Thyatira

The church there became so obscure that critics of Revelation argued that the book was suspect because there was never a church located at Thyatira – and this in AD200, just 100 years after they got mail.

Some believe that the church continued its obsession with weird, unbalanced prophecy, becoming a centre for the Montanist movement towards the end of the second century.

It seems that Thyatira got mail –and read it – but took little notice of what Christ said.

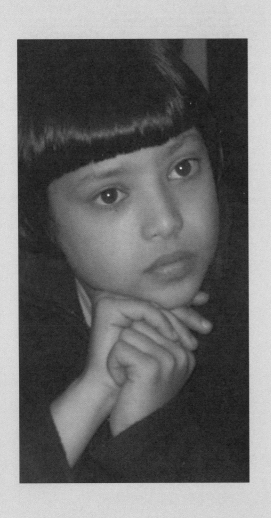

A LOYAL COMMUNITY

All that remains of Thyatira is modern-day Akhisar. The city occupied an important position in a corridor between two valleys.

MAIL FOR YOUR CHURCH

Designed for those in local church leadership, here are some questions to help you think through the implications of today's material for your congregation.

Faithful in Doctrine

What are the key facets of Christian doctrine that your church community views as central to its identity?

Look at this generationally. The reply will depend on the age of who is asked. There is less importance placed on forming an allegiance to a particular tradition and a growing emphasis on what actually goes on at a particular church and what's on offer.

▶ What is it that makes your church theologically distinctive from others in the area?

▶ Has the church changed in its view of doctrine in any way over the last 10 years?

▶ How would you judge this?

▶ Have some things become less important and others more?

▶ When considering services in the church, what aspect of the time together is viewed as most important – communion, the sermon, a time that is unstructured, or prayer?

▶ What are the benefits and challenges of our present position?

▶ How does the view on doctrine affect the church in action in the wider community?

▶ What are the main influences theologically in your church – is there one strong voice or do you have a diversity of voices?

Depending on the church context there are close links between a church's view on tradition and on Christian doctrine. How does the church address that relationship between these areas and what are the strengths and the challenges? Is there an emphasis on the work of the Holy Spirit, is there a strong view on the role of women, the inclusion and importance given to young people, the centrality of the communion or the time spent in worship or teaching?

GETTING THERE

These questions are taken from *Getting There*, a new Spring Harvest book by Ruth Dearnley. It is a book full of questions, to be used by anyone and in any church that's open to fresh challenge and serious thinking about the future.

Some questions are general. Others apply to specific situations and challenges. Some you have asked yourself. Others are asking things in a different way.

Ruth writes; "Questions are crucial to our growing together. We need to ask them and listen to each other's answers – not to force a decision but to learn what it is that joins us, what

we misunderstand and why we choose to go in a particular direction."

Getting There is on sale at Spring Harvest 2002. It is a practical book to be dipped into or worked through over a period of time. It is for all those involved in the leadership and management of the church. It is essential for anyone who wants to ask the questions that inform the way ahead.

Take it home and give it to those who have not been at Spring Harvest so that a church can talk together. You don't even have to have attended the event for it to work.

A LOYAL COMMUNITY

Faithful in Ethics and Integrity

▶ What is the church's understanding and approach to the Christian quality of holiness? Is holiness being loyal to the ways things are done; being morally pure; experiencing the power and the gifts of the Holy Spirit; or understanding grace?

▶ Is your accepted view of holiness attainable and how do you achieve it?

▶ When the church has to talk about or deal with ethical situations is it seen by church members as acting fairly?

▶ What vocabulary is used when talking about right and wrong?

Faithful to the Prophetic

▶ Is prophecy a word that is used in your church?

▶ If it's often used, is it useful?

▶ If it's not used at all, what do people see it as?

▶ How does the gift of prophecy contribute to the church's life in worship and mission?

▶ Is it happening but is talked about using other language such as 'someone had a thought or an idea'.

Women in Leadership

▶ When, in the life of the church, did women take a leading role?

▶ How has the view of women in leadership changed in your church over the last ten years?

▶ How can this continue to be developed?

▶ Who can be an effective help in this?

▶ Is there a balanced staff team – does it reflect the community you serve?

▶ How are people encouraged to follow their calling to leadership/ordination according to the tradition?

▶ Is there a gap in the team?

▶ Is there someone who could be encouraged to take the next step?

MARRIAGE ZONE

Questions to apply today's material to marriage

1. What is faithfulness – and how is it maintained?
2. How much of a part does the discovery and application of scripture play in your home and family?
3. What is your approach to guidance, 'God speaking' and decision making in your marriage? How do you think headship operates?
4. You've lost that loving feeling. What happens when the initial romance fades?

Journeying with Jesus

You've got MaiL

Jesus writes to his church

NOTES

Daily Menu

A long suffering community

The Christian life is a battle: John's Revelation gives us a behind-the-scenes glimpse of the ongoing conflict between good and evil being played out on earth. Suffering is part of that war, but is experienced in the context of hope for the final order and consummation of Christ's kingdom in eternity.

Bible passages

Zone outline

Church audit

Evening Celebration

Luke 23:26–43, Jesus on the cross.
The supreme place of suffering and triumph.

Jesus writes to his church

BIBLE PASSAGE

REVELATION

2:8–11   Smyrna

[8]"To the angel of the church in Smyrna write:

These are the words of him who is the First and the Last, who died and came to life again. [9]I know your afflictions and your poverty—yet you are rich! I know the slander of those who say they are Jews and are not, but are a synagogue of Satan. [10]Do not be afraid of what you are about to suffer. I tell you, the devil will put some of you in prison to test you, and you will suffer persecution for ten days. Be faithful, even to the point of death, and I will give you the crown of life.

[11]He who has an ear, let him hear what the Spirit says to the churches. He who overcomes will not be hurt at all by the second death."

3:7–13   Philadelphia

[7]"To the angel of the church in Philadelphia write:

These are the words of him who is holy and true, who holds the key of David. What he opens no-one can shut, and what he shuts no-one can open. [8]I know your deeds. See, I have placed before you an open door that no-one can shut. I know that you have little strength, yet you have kept my word and have not denied my name. [9]I will make those who are of the synagogue of Satan, who claim to be Jews though they are not, but are liars—I will make them come and fall down at your feet and acknowledge that I have loved you. [10]Since you have kept my command to endure patiently, I will also keep you from the hour of trial that is going to come upon the whole world to test those who live on the earth.

[11]I am coming soon. Hold on to what you have, so that no one will take your crown. [12]Him who overcomes I will make a pillar in the temple of my God. Never again will he leave it. I will write on him the name of my God and the name of the city of my God, the new Jerusalem, which is coming down out of heaven from my God; and I will also write on him my new name. [13]He who has an ear, let him hear what the Spirit says to the churches.

NOTES

Journeying with Jesus

YOU've got MaiL

Jesus writes to his church

Aims of this session:

■ Show that Christ praises these two churches without reservation – even though they are imperfect. He is the One who is perfect but not always taking issue with us

■ See that suffering is, far from being unusual, a normal part of the Christian experience

■ Ask questions about the so-called 'prosperity gospel' and other suggestions that Christianity is the pathway to guaranteed health and material gain

■ See that we perhaps need to gain more of an eternal perspective

■ Alert us to the plight of the contemporary suffering church

■ Ask questions about success, suffering and opportunity – and to evaluate what doors Christ might have already opened to us and to our churches

THE CHURCH – A LONG SUFFERING COMMUNITY

Smyrna

Two very different cities. One – Smyrna (now called Izmir) – was a beautiful jewel of a place known as *To Agalma tes Asias* (The Delight of Asia). It was and is still today a deep-water port; its inhabitants enjoyed wide, expansive streets, and the largest public theatre in Asia Minor. Smyrna proudly announced that it was the birthplace of Homer by stamping his image on its coins; it was the Stratford upon Avon of Asia.

The citizens of this fair city loved to stroll down Golden Street, a road that began at the sea, where the Temple of Cybele sat, and ended in the foothills at the Temple of Zeus. In taking that stroll they would pass impressive temples dedicated to Apollo, Asklepios and Aphrodite. The whole city was a model of meticulous town planning; it was built around the 4th century BC, and was home to around 100,000 people. It enjoyed a flourishing trade in wines, and was also famous for its science and medicine.

Philadelphia

Sixty miles east of Smyrna lay the new city of Philadelphia. If Smyrna was Stratford upon Avon, then Philadelphia was Milton Keynes or Harlow! The city had originally been built as a mission outpost for Greek culture and civilization; it sat on the borders of Mysia, Lydia and Phrygia, and was the last bastion of Greek thinking before the wilderness of the barbarians began. The city was built with the objective of converting the barbarians of Phrygia to the Greek way of thinking – a mission that had been singularly unsuccessful.

The close proximity of the city to a volcano was both good news and bad news. The soil was ideal for vines, and so Philadelphia was renowned worldwide for its vintages. The volcano also provided hot springs, where the sick were brought to bathe in its soothing waters.

SMYRNA

The beautiful Smyrna had itself been raised from the dead. Destroyed by an earthquake 600 years before Christ, the city had been a desolate ruin for three hundred years.

The citizens of Smyrna were politically astute – they always chose the right side in civil wars. They built a temple in 195BC to *Dea Roma* (Rome personified as a goddess) and had developed a reputation for patriotic loyalty to the Roman Empire. They competed in AD25 for the privilege to build a temple to Emperor Tiberius (many cities clamoured for the honour) and their bid alone succeeded. Their loyalty to Rome had been richly rewarded, they were an assize city and had been granted status as a free city as well. Smyrna was a keen rival to Ephesus, which sat thirty-five miles away to the South. It liked to think of itself as 'the first city'; first in loyalty to Rome, first in literary and cultural pedigree, and first in architectural beauty. One writer described it as 'a paradise of municipal vanity'. The city had built extensively on the summit of Mount Pagus, giving it the appearance of a crown when viewed from a distance. The crown was a symbol often to be found on coins. Modern Izmir has a population of around 250,000.

PHILADELPHIA

When the church there received mail from Christ, the city was experiencing problems with its Roman masters. Emperor Domitian had ordered the destruction of half of the vineyards – probably in an attempt to stimulate corn production. This was a devastating blow for Philadelphia, where the volcanic soils so ideal for wine were not so suitable for corn growth.

Philadelphia was very pagan – there were so many gods worshipped there that it was known as little Athens; the principal god was, unsurprisingly, Dionysius, the god of wine. Philadelphia was also the site of famous athletic games in honour of Zeus and Anaeitis.

Smyrna

To the angel of the church in
Smyrna write.

Rev 2:8

"Grace extends over every part
of (Smyrna) like a rainbow;
brightness reaches up towards the
skies, like the glitter of the bronze
of armour in Homer's epics."

– Aelius Aristides, second century orator and
resident of Smyrna

"Smyrna – one of the most
prosperous cities in Asia Minor."

– R.H. Charles

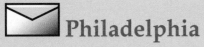Philadelphia

To the angel of the church in
Philadelphia write:

Rev 3:7

But the volcano meant very real danger too. It was so close, and new
cracks were said to appear every day in the walls of buildings. The
entire city had been completely devastated by an earthquake in AD17
and rebuilt courtesy of Roman tax concessions. After the rebuilding,
Philadelphia took a new name, Neocaesarea (new city of Caesar) –
although it reverted back to its old name within a couple of decades.
The volcano meant that the citizens of Philadelphia lived very unsettled lives – when the tremors came, they would flee for their life –
and there was a lot of 'going out and coming in', which was alluded
to by Christ in his words to the church there.

The churches

We don't really know how the church got started in Smyrna. It is
not mentioned in Acts or in the New Testament epistles; an early
tradition states that Paul visited the city on his way to Ephesus at
the beginning of his third missionary journey. Some suggest that
the church was started by a Jew present in Jerusalem on the day of
Pentecost (Acts 2:9). There is also a tradition that the apostle John
visited the city.

Polycarp, a disciple of the apostle John, was leader of the church for
many years: he would have been in his twenties when he assumed
leadership there. Polycarp, like old John, had no time for heretics;
it is said that one day, when John was bathing in the public baths,
a heretic by the name of Cerinthus entered the baths – whereupon
John called upon all the Christians to evacuate the area in order
to avoid the lightning bolt of judgement that he thought might be
imminent!

Polycarp himself had to confront Marcion, a wealthy shipowner
who tried to 'cleanse' Christianity of all that was Jewish (he rejected
the narratives of Christ's birth, and only accepted the letters of Paul
– and even then rejected the letters to Timothy and Titus). Polycarp's
personality is revealed by the way that he described Marcion, greeting him face to face as 'the first-born of Satan'.

We know even less about the origins of the Philadelphian church.
It was possibly a church plant from Smyrna, or from Colossae,
Laodicea or Hierapolis. Ignatius stayed there while under arrest and
on his way to Rome; the church had a bishop, as well as presbyters
and deacons. It was quite a small church when it received mail from
Jesus.

Overlooking Smyrna towards the sea.

Philadelphia, sitting at the open door of a very fertile tract of land.

Journeying with Jesus

YOU've got MaiL

Jesus writes to his church

Opposition

There were very significant Jewish communities in Smyrna and Philadelphia – and they were very hostile to the Nazarenes (Christians). The opposition was official; anti-Christian curses were inserted into the Jewish liturgy. As we have already seen, this was most likely because:

- ✉ Christians were trying to evangelize Jews
- ✉ The Jews saw as blasphemous the worship of a crucified criminal as Messiah
- ✉ Christians were attempting to shelter under the legislative umbrella enjoyed by Jews, meaning that they did not have to offer sacrifices to the Roman emperor.

Just as Satan is the accuser, so false accusations were being levelled at the Christians by the Jewish communities – and so, according to Christ, both cities have 'synagogues of Satan' in them. Ultimately it would be Jewish voices, together with those of the pagans, which would call for the execution of Polycarp of Smyrna. It would seem that believers in the cities were being subjected to, among other things, mob rule and attacks on their property together with imprisonment and the threat of death (prison was not part of punishment in those days – it was simply a holding area until trial or execution).

John – himself a Jew – sees Jewishness not in racial or ethnic terms, but as describing those people who are faithful to God (Rom 2:28,29).

For some Christians, the challenge of 'taking the pinch' (an annual vow where every Roman citizen would burn a pinch of incense on an altar to Caesar) would signal the threat of persecution. This was more of a test of political loyalty than religious orthodoxy; but everyone who had passed the pinch test carried a certificate; the lack of a certificate meant that you were branded as a disloyal and disaffected citizen, an outlaw. The Christians routinely refused – and were denied the certificates; this meant that they lived with the constant threat that persecution was just around the corner. They lived every day as those staring into the unknown.

> **Press to reply**
>
> **What are the pinch tests in your own experience – moments when you are called upon to conform to what everybody else is doing, but where you know that to 'take the pinch' means disloyalty to Jesus?**

"Philadelphia – a city full of earthquakes, for the walls never cease being cracked, and different parts of the city are constantly suffering damage. That is why the actual town has few inhabitants, but the majority live as farmers in the countryside, as they have fertile land. But one is surprised even at the few, that they are as fond of the place when they have such insecure dwellings."

– Strabo

"Philadelphia was founded to make it a centre of the Graeco-Asiatic civilization and a means of spreading the Greek language and manners in the eastern parts of Lydia and in Phrygia. It was a missionary city in the beginning."

– Sir William Ramsay

 Smyrna

I know the slander of those who say they are Jews and are not, but are a synagogue of Satan.

Rev 2:9

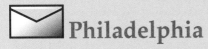 Philadelphia

I will make those who are of the synagogue of Satan, who claim to be Jews though they are not, but are liars – I will make them come and fall down at your feet and acknowledge that I have loved you.

Rev 3:9

AT A PINCH

Once a year the Roman citizen had to burn a pinch of incense on the altar to the godhead of Caesar; and, having done so, he was given a certificate to guarantee that he had performed his religious duty. We possess a request for and a specimen of such a certificate.

The request runs:

"To those who have been appointed to preside over the sacrifices, from Inares Akeus, from the village of Theoxenis, together with his children Aias and Hera, who reside in the village of Theadelphia. We have always sacrificed to the gods, and now, in your presence, according to the regulations, we have sacrificed and offered libations, and tasted the sacred things, and we ask you to give us a certification that we have done so. May you fare well."

The certificate itself runs:

"We, the representatives of the emperor, Serenos and Hermas, have seen you sacrificing."

Then follows the date. Every Roman citizen had to make that sacrifice and receive that certificate.

One thing is clear. The burning of this pinch of incense was obviously not a test of a man's religious orthodoxy; it was a test of his political loyalty. In point of fact the Roman government was extremely tolerant. Once a man had made his sacrifice and received his certificate, he could go and worship any god or goddess he liked, provided that worship did not conflict with public decency and order. But if he refused to burn that pinch of incense, he was by his refusal automatically branded as a disloyal and disaffected citizen. With an empire the size of the Roman Empire, no government could afford to have disaffected citizens, who might become storm centres of trouble. Therefore any man who refused to burn his pinch of incense was rendered by his very refusal an outlaw.

All that the Christians had to do was to burn that pinch of incense, say, 'Caesar is Lord', receive their certificate and go away and worship as they pleased. But that is precisely what the Christians would not do. They would give to no man the name of Lord; that name they would keep for Jesus Christ and Jesus Christ alone. They would not even formally conform. Uncompromisingly the Christians refused to go through the forms of Caesar worship, and therefore the Christians were outlaws, and liable to persecution at any time. Persecution was not continuous, but it was liable to break out at any time, for informers were frequent and numerous. The Christian was like a man over whose head the sword of execution was constantly poised, and he never knew when it might fall, for the Roman government regarded his refusal to conform as the act of a dangerous and disloyal citizen.

Nowhere can life have been more dangerous for a Christian than in Smyrna.

– William Barclay

Jesus writes to his church

"May the Nazarenes and the minim [heretics] perish in a moment, and be blotted out from the book of life, and with the righteous may they not be inscribed. Blessed art Thou, O Lord, Who humblest the arrogant."

– excerpt from The Eighteen Benedictions *(synagogue prayers used every Sabbath that were designed to curse the early Christians)*

"In Smyrna the church was a place for heroes."

– William Barclay

"There were Christians in Smyrna who were men of such heroic calibre that the word of the Risen Christ to them was a word of unadulterated praise. In a city where the splendour of heathen worship might well have suffocated the life out of the Christian Church, in a city where the pride of men looked on the humble Christians with arrogant contempt, in a city where every Christian was between the devil of the demands of Caesar worship and the deep sea of Jewish slander and malignancy, there were Christians who were faithful unto death."

– William Barclay

Nothing but praise

Of the seven churches that got mail from Christ, only two received no words of criticism at all; Smyrna and Philadelphia. They were singled out for words of encouragement and commendation alone. This demonstrates a very important point about the nature of Christ himself.

There is no suggestion the lack of criticism means these two churches were perfect; they both comprised fallen human beings, so there were surely flaws and faults.

What we do see is that Christ is not a fault-finding, picky character who can never be pleased or satiated. On the contrary, he chooses to be silent about things that he could have easily found fault with.

virus warning **CRITICISM OR PRAISE**
Some feel that following Jesus is so demanding he will always automatically have issues of criticism about our lives. Apparently, we are wrong. Even though we are far from perfect, there are times when Christ offers only praise.

 Press to reply

Why do some of us feel that he is the God who can never really be pleased or satisfied with us?

Suffering

Christ sends encouraging mail to two churches that are going through a very hard time of suffering; there are some vital lessons to be learned about suffering from his words.

virus warning **PRINCIPLES OF PAIN**
Bear in mind that the problem of pain and suffering is very complex; our study here will not attempt to wrestle with the issue at depth, and we should always avoid thoughtless or clichéd responses to those who wrestle with suffering. But there are some helpful foundational principles that emerge.

1. Suffering is part of the normal Christian life

Nowhere does Scripture suggest Christians will experience freedom from suffering. On the contrary, the Bible makes it very clear that suffering and trials are part of the life of faith – and this was particularly

Journeying with Jesus

You've got MaiL

Jesus writes to his church

"The world must get out of the cloister and into the world ... where man is challenged to participate in the sufferings of God at the hands of a godless world. He must therefore plunge himself into the life of a godless world without attempting to gloss over its ungodliness with a veneer of religion or trying to transfigure it. He must live a worldly life and so participate in the suffering of God."

– *Dietrich Bonhoeffer*

 Smyrna

These are the words of him who is the First and the Last, who died and came to life again. I know your afflictions and your poverty – yet you are rich!

Rev 2:8

"Conflict is the inevitable result of Christian authenticity in John's view."

– *Jonathan Knight*

"Christ promised his people three things – that they would be in constant trouble; that they would be completely fearless; and that they would be completely happy."

– *W.R. Maltby*

demonstrated in the lives of the early Christians (2 Cor 1:6, 8:2, Phil 1:29, James 1:12, 1 Pet 1:6, 3:14, 4:12). Christ's promise to keep the Philadelphians from a worldwide persecution should not suggest they would avoid it – we know that for a historical fact. Rather he promised to offer them grace in it, to keep them from buckling under pressure.

The believers who lived in Smyrna and Philadelphia knew suffering as a daily reality. They experienced:

- **Tribulation**. The Greek word is *thlipsis*, which means pressure; and in classical Greek it is always used in its literal sense. It is used, for instance, to describe the plight of a man who was tortured to death by being slowly crushed by a great boulder laid upon him.

- **Poverty**. The word used for poverty is *ptocheia*, which means destitution. In Greek, there are two words for poverty. One describes the poverty of the man who has to work for a living, the poverty of the person who has nothing superfluous. But the other, the word used in addressing the Smyrnian church, describes the poverty of the person who has nothing at all. Generally speaking, the early Christians were poor (1 Cor 1:26,27, James 2:5). Smyrna was one of the wealthiest of cities, and Roman thinking clearly suggested that to be poor meant that you were of absolutely no consequence, so it must have been very hard for the believers to suffer in this way. Their poverty may have come from a combination of their background prior to coming to Christ, coupled with hardship following their conversion, perhaps because their homes were plundered (Heb 10:34).

virus warning   **DISCIPLESHIP AND RICHES**

The notion that Christian discipleship is a way to personal riches, or a life undisturbed by sickness is a grave error. And the reverse of this, that Christ cannot heal or provide is also error.

- **Slander**. Christians were being accused of the most appalling crimes, and all because perfectly innocent ideas, like the brotherhood/sisterhood of believers and the eucharist, were being made to sound as if incest and cannibalism were common practice among the Nazarenes. Talk of loving one's brother or sister and of eating Christ's body and drinking his blood was used to fuel the slander. A few years after Smyrna got mail from Christ, the Roman governor of Bithynia, Pliny, assumed that these crimes were being committed. Even though Pliny

SUFFERING IN OLD AND NEW TESTAMENT THINKING

Old Testament

The Semitic mind dealt with concrete situations rather than abstract forms. Their perspective was not to treat the issue of suffering as an intellectual one. The Old Testament writers, accordingly, sought to identify the causes and purposes of suffering when it happened.

The Hebrews regarded suffering as punishment for sin against the divine moral order. The wicked would surely suffer for their evil ways (Psa 7:15, 16, 37:1–3, 73:12–20, 139:19), even though they might prosper for a time (Job 21:28–33). Some writers expressed consternation that God stayed his hand of judgment against the offenders of his will (Jer 12:1–4; Hab 1:2–4; Mal 3:7–15). They often interpreted their own suffering as a sign of God's wrath and punishment for sin in their lives. The highly developed sense of corporate identity in Hebrew thought meant that suffering could come as a result of parents' sin (1 Kings 21:20,22,29; an idea reflected by Jesus' disciples in John 9:2, the story of the healing of the man born blind) or the wickedness of the king (2 Kings 21:10,11).

The suffering of the righteous posed a problem. It was explained variously as a way for God to gain people's attention (Job 33:14, 36:15), to correct sin into obedience (2 Chron 20:9,10; Mal 3:3), to develop or refine character (Job 23:10; Psa 66:10). Ultimately, the writers consigned themselves to trust in God's sometimes hidden wisdom (Job 42:2, 3; Psa 135:6).

The prophet gained a vision of a greater purpose in suffering – carrying the sins of others (Isa 53). As eschatological hopes matured in late Old Testament and intertestamental times, the righteous looked forward to the Day of the Lord when they would be vindicated and justice would reign (Dan 12:1).

Suffering rightly responded to can lead to a deeper relationship with God (Job 42:4–6; Pas 73:21–26).

New Testament

Into an evil world God sent his only Son. God is himself touched by the suffering of Christ on the cross. Christian writers in the New Testament incorporated the trials of Christ into their existing Old Testament understanding of suffering. The purposefulness and necessity of suffering in the life of the Son of God (Matt 16:21; Mark 8:31; Luke 9:22) aided them in coping with their own. One aspect of God's purpose for us in suffering is the development of a godly, Christ-like character (Rom 8:28–29; 2 Peter 1:3–8).

The early Christians recognized the inevitability of their suffering. As Christ suffered, so would they (John 16:33; Acts 14:22; Rom 8:31–39; 1 Cor 12:26; 1 Thess 2:14; 2 Tim 3:12; 1 Pet 4:12,13). Continuing his mission, they would incur tribulation (Mark 13:12,13; Rev 17:6, 20:14) because the world hates the disciples as much as it did their Lord (see John 15:18; 1 Cor 2:8; 1 John 3:11,12). Suffering for his sake was counted a privilege (Acts 5:41; 1 Cor 11:32; 1 Thess 1:4–8).

New Testament writers realized there were other types of suffering than that incurred as they lived on Christian mission. These are to be endured patiently rather than rebelliously (1 Thess 3:3; James 1:2–4) because God is working his purpose out in his children's lives (Rom 8:28–29). Satan would tempt believers to be defeated in their suffering (2 Cor 4:8–12; Rev 2:10). Instead, Christians can grow stronger spiritually through trials (Rom 6:4–8; 1 Pet 4:1; Heb 12:11) and share Christ's ultimate triumph (Mark 13:9; John 16:33; 2 Thess 1:5; Rev 5:5; 20:9,14,15) even now as they experience daily victories (Rom 8:37; 1 John 2:13–14; 1 Pet 5:10). Therefore, sufferings give rise to hope (Rom 12:12; 1 Thess 1:3), for no present suffering compares with the rewards that await the faithful follower of Christ (Rom 8:17–18).

– *T.R. McNeal,* Holman Bible Dictionary

Smyrna

Do not be afraid of what you are about to suffer. I tell you, the devil will put some of you in prison to test you, and you will suffer persecution for ten days.

Rev 2:10

Philadelphia

I know that you have little strength, yet you have kept my word and have not denied my name. ... Since you have kept my command to endure patiently, I will also keep you from the hour of trial that is going to come upon the whole world to test those who live on the earth.

Rev 3:8,10

"Dear friends, do not be surprised at the painful trial you are suffering, as though something strange were happening to you. But rejoice that you participate in the sufferings of Christ, so that you may be overjoyed when his glory is revealed. If you are insulted because of the name of Christ, you are blessed, for the Spirit of glory and of God rests on you. If you suffer, it should not be as a murderer or thief or any other kind of criminal, or even as a meddler. However, if you suffer as a Christian, do not be ashamed, but praise God that you bear that name."

– 1 Pet 4:12–16

thoroughly investigated the rumours and found them to be false, the rumours and urban myths continued. The Jews often had the ear of the powerful (Nero was turned against Christians by two Jewish proselytes). As Barclay says, "The Jews whispered their slanders against the Christians into the ears of the Roman authorities with calculated and poisonous venom."

virus ⚠ **warning** 🕷 **BEWARE YOUR BIAS**
None of the above should be construed as any kind of anti-Semitism. People calling themselves Christians have been guilty of some of the worst atrocities of history – and we must face that fact. These statements cannot be perceived as anti-Jewish in any sense; they are simply historical reality about certain individuals who were from a Jewish background. Christ is unafraid to unmask the reality of the situation with the use of language like 'the synagogue of Satan.'

Press to reply

Have there been times in your own experience when slanderous accusations have been made about you or your church because of your love for Christ? How did you respond?

Suffering is normal – and not just in the past

Suffering for Christ is not just a historic reality – we tend to have a blinkered view as we live in relative ease: but there are many faithful believers around the world who are suffering loss of livelihood, separation from family, imprisonment, torture and death for the cause of the gospel. The shocking fact is that:

- ✉ In 1996, a staggering 159,000 martyrs died for Christ around the world
- ✉ In 1999, the number had risen to 164,000 cases of Christian martyrdom worldwide.

For the Christian, suffering is not limited to opposition and persecution. Christians suffer with health problems, experience tragedy, walk through financial challenges, and ultimately, if Christ tarries, will die. There is not a hint in the mail from Jesus that we will in any way be exempted from the normal bruises that life brings. But we are promised God's strength, grace, and ultimate victory over death through the triumph of Christ.

A LONG SUFFERING COMMUNITY

MODERN MARTYRS

"Suffering plays a major part in the life of the world church today. In David Barrett's annual update of the statistics of world Christianity, he includes a column for Christian martyrs. How many Christians do you think died for their faith in 1996? Twenty or thirty? A hundred maybe? The answer is a staggering 159,000 (the statistics for 1999, the latest available, show the annual figure as 164,000). Following Jesus is not a soft option. That ought not to surprise us. Do you think Jesus himself was a successful man? If he were here today, who would sponsor his ministry? Jesus offers a hard challenge: "Take up your cross and follow me" (Mark 8:34). Yet it is a challenge with a promise. For those who will follow, Jesus offers a dynamic vision with the potential to change the whole of life. Our personal thinking, our feelings, our relationships, our emotions – these are all included. Moreover, this vision goes beyond the needs of individuals, and ultimately offers the possibility of transformation for the whole cosmos, embraced by a spirituality that is vibrant and alive. It is a vision in which the wounded and broken hearted are lifted up, in which those who are nobodies can become somebody, where new communities can create community amongst the most unlikely of folk, as ordinary people empowered by God's spirit find themselves able to do extraordinary things. To those who share this vision, and who would like to see the world this way, Jesus' call is as vital and relevant as it ever was: Come and take up your cross, and follow me. Bring the baggage of your own life, whatever it might be – for that is part of the cross we bear – and join him on the journey towards personal and cultural transformation and fulfilment. It is not an easy pathway, it might even be painful, and we can only decide for ourselves whether it is worth the cost."

– John Drane

"Blessed is the man who perseveres under trial, because when he has stood the test, he will receive the crown of life that God has promised to those who love him."

– James 1:12

"For our light and momentary troubles are achieving for us an eternal glory that far outweighs them all. So we fix our eyes not on what is seen, but on what is unseen. For what is seen is temporary, but what is unseen is eternal."

– 2 Cor 4:17

"Blessed are you when people insult you, persecute you and falsely say all kinds of evil against you because of me. Rejoice and be glad, because great is your reward in heaven, for in the same way they persecuted the prophets who were before you."

– Matt 5:11–12

"I have served him for eighty-six years, and he has done me no wrong; how then can I blaspheme the King who saved me?"

– Polycarp of Smyrna, replying when commanded to renounce Christ

2. Face suffering with an eternal perspective

The mail to the seven churches is designed to comfort and exhort believers who are living in the crucible of pressure with the news that:

- ☒ Ultimately Christ, not Caesar, controls history
- ☒ Behind their daily battle rages an invisible battle between the forces of good and evil
- ☒ Christ stands as the comprehensive victor astride death and hell
- ☒ Every letter contains the promise of the victor's reward. These promises are metaphorical and symbolic, but all are eschatological ("The part of theology concerned with death and final destiny." *Oxford English Reference Dictionary*) in nature and correspond with the last two chapters of the book of Revelation. The reference "eat from the tree of life" (Rev 2:7) is parallel to the tree of life in Rev 22:2, and obviously echoes back to Eden (Gen 2–3). What was lost in Adam is more than regained in Christ. The future is stunningly bright for the presently beleaguered believers.

Compared with the vista of eternity, the New Testament writers were able to see the trials of this life in the context of being 'momentary' (2 Cor 4:17) as part of a life where "you are a mist that appears for a little while and then vanishes" (James 4:14). Christ is coming back "in just a very little while" (Heb 10:37). Paul struggled with a genuine dilemma of remaining on earth to continue ministry or departing quickly to be with Christ forever (Phil 1:21). Eternity loomed large in the thinking of the early Christians.

The story of the death of Smyrna's leader, Polycarp, opens to public view the private forces working powerfully in the hearts of courageous believers. The Martyrdom of Polycarp, the oldest non-biblical account of a martyr's death, was written soon after his murder in 156 to strengthen faith in time of persecution. The story is somewhat embellished by miraculous happenings, such as so much blood spurting from a wound in Polycarp's side that it extinguished the fire consuming him. What is certain is that the now-elderly leader refused to compromise and paid the ultimate price for his faith.

- ☒ Polycarp's pastorate at Smyrna was lengthy, and he invested a lot of time in the youth to raise up leaders who would follow after him
- ☒ When Polycarp was 86 years old, the expected storm finally broke for both Smyrna and Philadelphia
- ☒ Some believers were publicly tortured to death; Germanicus

DO YOU DESERVE TO BE HAPPY?

Should a Christian who is faithful to the Lord enjoy a happy, generally successful and secure life? "Yes," we reply, without much hesitation; which only goes to show how deeply we are infected by the spirit of our culture rather than by the witness of God's word. The plain truth is that the Bible represents the life of faith as a generally hard, unrewarding and even painful experience. Jesus spoke of it in terms of a cross, with all that this implied in the first-century world. Indeed it would not be overstating the case to say that the Bible knows almost nothing of the happy, successful, carefree believer, or if it does, his existence is something of an enigma (Matt 19:24) explicable only in terms of the mystery of God's grace. Jesus' terms of discipleship are harsh in the extreme (Luke 14:25–35). Suffering is an essential ingredient of the Christian life according to the unanimous testimony of the New Testament.

TRIAL BEFORE RUSTICUS

Justin Martyr was converted to Christ around AD130. He taught in Ephesus and later opened a Christian school in Rome. He and some of his friends were denounced as Christians in around AD165 – they were scourged and then beheaded when they refused to bow the knee to the emperor. Here is part of the account of his cross examination at trial before Rusticus, the prefect of Rome, where Justin was asked to explain the beliefs of Christians:

Justin: We profess concerning the Christian God that he is One, eternal from the beginning, the Creator of all that exists, seen and unseen. We also believe in his Son, our Lord Jesus Christ, whose coming as the Saviour of mankind was foretold by the ancient prophets.

Prefect: You are said to be a learned man. Do you really believe that if you are scourged and beheaded, you will go up to heaven?

Justin: I trust that I shall be given the grace of God to endure such things. I know that for all who so live, grace remains until the end of the world.

Prefect: Do you then think that you will go up to heaven to receive rewards from above?

Justin: I don't think, I know, I am fully persuaded.

Prefect: All right. Let's turn to the matter in hand. Will you agree to make sacrifice to the gods?

Justin: No one who is right-minded would turn from the truth to falsehood.

Prefect: If you do not obey, you will be punished without mercy.

Justin: If we are punished for the sake of our Lord Jesus Christ we expect to be saved, for this will give us confidence before the more terrible judgment seat of our Lord and Saviour, on the day that he judges the whole world. You must do what you will. We are Christians and will not offer sacrifices to idols.

At this point Rusticus gave sentence and the martyrs were led away to the customary place and beheaded, 'fulfilling their witness by confessing their saviour.'

– Acta Sancti Justini et Sociorum (The Acts of Saint Justin and His Companions)

"To maintain one's faith while enduring insults and suffering persecution for a prolonged period is more difficult than standing for the truth by laying down one's life. In order to achieve the latter it is necessary only to be strong and courageous for one day. But to endure ridicule, hostility and persecution constantly – to reproduce the strength and courage of one day for months or years or even tens of years – that requires even greater faith and courage and an even higher level of obedience."

– Wang Mingdao, a Chinese Christian leader imprisoned for twenty-three years after the Communists came to power

 Smyrna

Be faithful, even to the point of death, and I will give you the crown of life. He who has an ear, let him hear what the Spirit says to the churches. He who overcomes will not be hurt at all by the second death.

Rev 2:10

was thrown to the beasts – but Quintus caved in when faced with the beasts and offered a sacrifice to the emperor

- ⊠ Eleven Christians had died, but this was not enough for the gathered crowd. They called for Polycarp, who was tracked down at a little farm in the hills

- ⊠ Polycarp welcomed his arresters, offering them food and drink. He was brought before the officials and pressed to deny Christ, which he refused to do. He was then taken to the stadium at Smyrna, invited again to swear by the genius of Caesar and say 'away with the atheists' (Christians were described as atheists because they had no visible object of worship). Polycarp looked at the pagans in the crowd and, gesturing to them, said 'away with the atheists'

- ⊠ No lions were available for Polycarp to be thrown to, so he was burnt to death – eye witnesses said the Jews in the crowd were especially keen to help build the fire. Polycarp was burned alive, and finally stabbed to death

- ⊠ The congregation at Smyrna celebrated the anniversary of Polycarp's death as his birthday in later years. For the early believers, death was just birth into the joys of eternity with the risen Christ.

virus ⚠warning  **WATCH OUT FOR ETERNITY**
Perhaps we are nervous of a gospel message that focuses too much on the life to come: we want to ensure that we are 'not too heavenly minded to be of any earthly use' and that our message is not just 'pie in the sky when we die.' But Christ's mail to the seven churches makes it apparent that a clear sense of heaven and the eternal is vital if we are to negotiate the trials of life this side of eternity.

Press to reply

Is it possible that we veer sometimes to the extreme of being 'too earthly minded to be of any heavenly use?'

3. Suffering does not mean desertion

We can be quick to assume that the advent of pain and suffering in our lives suggests that God has become distant, or perhaps deserted us completely. But the letters to these two suffering churches make it clear that although God is not the author of their pain he is fully aware of all they face. We must remember this when we face pain or opposition.

FACING OPPOSITION

Some Christians have to face constant opposition from the state authorities or from other religious groups, from people at work or within their own families. Some even find their lives in danger. For all of us there are periods when our faith is severely tested. How can we survive such pressure?

▶ Remember the words of the risen Christ: 'I know your afflictions' (Rev 2:9). Our situation does not catch him by surprise.

▶ Remember that Jesus not only knows but shares our suffering. At the heart of Christianity is the cross, which tells us that God has entered a suffering world, to suffer for us and with us. In the library of Corpus Christi College, Cambridge, is a rather dirty looking Bible that belonged to Thomas Bilney, a minor character of the English Reformation in the sixteenth century. He was no great hero and sometimes wavered in his faith. But in the end he was burnt at the stake for his commitment to the gospel. In his Bible, the verses which comforted him in his last days (in his version, in Latin) are heavily marked in ink: 'Fear not, for I have redeemed you; I have summoned you by name; you are mine ... . When you walk through the fire, you will not be burned; the flames will not set you ablaze. For I am the Lord, your God, the Holy One of Israel, your Saviour' (Isa 43:1–3).

▶ Give and receive encouragement from other Christians. 'Remember those in prison as if you were their fellow prisoners, and those who are ill-treated as if you yourselves were suffering' (Heb 13:3). 'Carry each other's burdens, and in this way you will fulfil the law of Christ' (Gal 6:2).

▶ Take encouragement from the words of Jesus, who lived as he taught: 'Bless those who curse you, pray for those who ill-treat you' (Luke 6:28). By an extraordinary irony of human experience it is often those who have suffered greatly who are most able to forgive. In 1943 Etty Hillesum, a Dutch Jew, was taken with her family to Auschwitz, where they all met their deaths. Despite the horror of the suffering she never gave in to hate. In her diary she commented how cruel and merciless the Nazis were, adding, 'We must be all the more merciful ourselves.'

▶ Pray for strength not to provoke by argument those who oppose you, but to live a deeply Christian life. 'Make every effort to live in peace with all men and to be holy' (Heb 12:14). 'Always be prepared to give an answer to everyone who asks you to give the reason for the hope that you have. But do this with gentleness and respect, keeping a clear conscience, so that those who speak maliciously against your good behaviour in Christ may be ashamed of their slander' (1 Peter 3:15–16).

▶ Remember that, for most of us, the Christian life is a marathon race, not a sprint. There is no quick escape from hardship. There is what has been called 'a long obedience in the same direction.'

– Stephen Travis

 Philadelphia

I am coming soon. Hold on to what you have, so that no one will take your crown. Him who overcomes I will make a pillar in the temple of my God. Never again will he leave it. I will write on him the name of my God and the name of the city of my God, the new Jerusalem, which is coming down out of heaven from my God; and I will also write on him my new name. He who has an ear, let him hear what the Spirit says to the churches.

Rev 3:11

"The last enemy to be destroyed is death. For he 'has put everything under his feet'."

– 1 Cor 15:26–27

www.24-7prayer.org

www
http//web link

www.persecution.org
(International Christian Concern)

www.persecution.com
(The Voice of The Martyrs)

www.vom.org
(The Voice of The Martyrs)

www.idop.org
(International Day of Prayer for the Persecuted Church)

www.persecutedchurch.org
(International Day of Prayer for the Persecuted Church)

www.jubileecampaign.co.uk
(Jubilee Campaign – human rights pressure group)

www.releaseinternational.org
Release International

www.csw.org.uk
Christian Solidarity Worldwide

www.od.org
Open Doors

Press to reply

Sometimes new Christians get discouraged when they go through trials and tragedy, feeling that perhaps God has abandoned them. What words of help would you give to someone struggling with those feelings?

Christ wants his suffering family to know:

- He knows all about their situation, and tells them the truth about the dangers that may lay ahead
- He encourages them to stand firm, encouraging them that there will be rewards for the faithful
- In Smyrna, the believers will be given a crown of life – the ultimate municipal accolade in that city – but it is Christ who rewards
- The Christians from Smyrna may see death, but will not be hurt by the 'second death' – the judgment of the wicked
- The believers at Philadelphia may find themselves excluded from the synagogue, but they serve the Christ who holds the key of David. This is a reference to Isaiah 22:22 where Eliakim, the faithful servant of King Hezekiah, holds the key of access to the royal house. Those excluded and scorned by evil men and women on earth are promised open access to the king's banquet
- Pillars and new names. Eminent citizens would often be honoured by the municipal authorities by the inscribing of their name on a temple pillar; here Christ alludes to this practice with the promise that those faithful to him will be so honoured among the people of God, the new temple (1 Cor 3:9, 16–17)
- Security forever. Philadelphia, the city that was always an earthquake fugitive, was full of 'going out and coming back' because of the daily tremors. But there is a promise that the believers will not have to leave the temple for any reason (Rev 3:12). This is a promise of ultimate safety; the person who knows that even death cannot threaten them has discovered the true peace that is vital for life today. The last enemy has been destroyed, and the believer no longer lives fearfully under its volcanic shadow
- Future vindication. One day the Christians of Philadelphia would discover that roles would be reversed between them and the persecuting Jews, who would "come and fall down at your feet and acknowledge that I have loved you" (Rev 3:9). This is not to suggest that the Jews would be forced into some kind of grovelling, and thus the Christians would have their day of vengeance, but rather is a reversal of the prophesies of Isaiah

WHAT HARM CAN A CHILD DO?

Linh Dao
Vietnam
1991

Four police officers suddenly burst into ten-year-old Linh Dao's home. They forced her father, an underground pastor in North Vietnam, to remain seated while the authorities ransacked the home searching for Bibles.

"I remember when the police came," Linh Dao recalls. "They searched around the house all of that morning and asked many different questions. It was scary to talk to the policemen, but I knew what they were looking for, so I concentrated and tried my best not to be scared or nervous." As the police questioned her parents, Linh courageously hid some of the Bibles in her school knapsack.

When the police asked her about the contents of the knapsack, Linh simply replied, "It is books for children."

Linh Dao's father was arrested that day and sentenced to seven years of re-education through hard labour.

"When the policemen decided to take my dad away, all of my family knelt down and prayed. I prayed first, then my sister, then my mum, and last of all, my dad. I prayed that my dad would have peace and remain healthy and that my family would survive these hard times. We were all crying, but I told myself I have to face what's happening now."

Word quickly spread about the arrest, and neighbouring children began to ask Linh what criminal acts her father had done. She told her friends, "My father is not a criminal. He is a Christian, and I am proud of him for not wavering in his faith!"

As each day passed, Linh Dao made a mark on her wooden bookcase as she prayed for her father. She remembers, "I cried almost every single night because I worried how my father was doing in prison and how the policemen were treating him.

"Before my dad was in prison, I was just a child. I didn't need to worry about anything. It was a lot different after my dad left. My mind got older very quickly. I told my sister that we had to help mum do the work around the house, so she could continue to do my dad's work in the church.

"I prayed every day and every night. My faith grew very fast. I knew one thing that I had to concentrate on and that was spending time learning from the Bible so when I grew up, I could be like my dad, sharing and preaching. When I think about this, I feel my heart burning inside me, pushing me, telling me this is the right thing to do."

Finally, after more than a year, Linh, her mother, and sister were able to visit their father in prison. When they reached the compound, they were separated by a chain fence. Linh quickly discovered that she could squeeze into the prison yard through a chained gate. She ran to her father and hugged him tightly. The guards watched the little girl but, surprisingly, left her alone. 'What harm can a little girl do?' they must have thought.

Little did they know! Armed with innocence and child-like faith, children are a secret weapon against the kingdom of Satan. During that first visit to her father's prison, Linh was able to smuggle him a pen, which he used to write scriptures and sermons on cigarette paper. These 'cigarette sermons' travelled from cell to cell and were instrumental in bringing many prisoners to Christ.

Linh Dao's prayers were answered. Her father was released early, before he had served all seven years of his sentence. "It was a big surprise when I came home from school one day and saw my dad had been released from prison. I ran and then gave him a big hug. We were so happy. I was proud of my family and I wanted to yell and let the whole world know that I wasn't scared of anything because God always protects each step I go in my life."

Linh Dao is now a teenager. She desires to follow in the footsteps of her father and be a preacher of the Gospel of Jesus Christ. She knows first hand the dangers of sharing her faith in Communist Vietnam and remains determined to obey Christ rather than men. In spite of a grim future, she spends her time in intense Bible study.

Jesus Freaks, DC Talk and the Voice of the Martyrs

CROWN OF LIFE

In verse 10 we have the famous phrase 'the crown of life'. The Greek word is *stephanos*. It is to be noted that in Greek stephanos is not the royal crown; that is *diadema*, from which the English word diadem comes. Stephanos has three main usages.

i. It is the crown of victory in the games, the wreath or laurel which was given to the athlete who overcame. The Christian is the athlete of God. The race may be long and hard; it may take all that a person has to give. The Christian is the one who is for ever pressing towards a goal. But the end of the struggle makes it worth it all.

ii. It is the festal crown that was worn at marriages and on other festal occasions. The Christian life is a life of joy now, and joy hereafter.

iii. In Smyrna this word *stephanos* would have both these meanings but it would have another meaning also. In Smyrna the reward for faithful municipal service was a laurel crown. On the coins of Smyrna it is common to see great and honoured magistrates so depicted and so crowned. If the Christian is to receive their reward, they must be faithful in the service of their brothers and sisters. He or she is in this world to serve.

– Adapted from William Barclay

(45:14, 49:6) that speak about Gentiles being accepted by Israel's God. Now, it is not the Gentile oppressors of Israel who must acknowledge their special place in God's plan, but Jewish persecutors who will acknowledge that the church, Jew and Gentile alike, is loved by God.

virus ⚠ warning 🕷 **ANTI-SEMITISM**
Christ is for all: there is not a shred of anti-Semitism here, but rather a joyful acknowledgement that Christ is the saviour of both the Jew and Gentile that acknowledges and calls upon his name for salvation.

4. Jesus measures success differently

The Sermon on the Mount shows that Christ established an upside-down kingdom – or perhaps we must say that his view is the right side up. He has a different value system, a radical view of evaluating success.

- ✉ The church at Smyrna was struggling financially, but Christ viewed it as rich – whereas the Laodiceans, who saw themselves as rich, were poor, blind and naked
- ✉ The church at Philadelphia was small and weak – yet had an open door.

While we don't to make poverty a virtue – and sometimes small churches justify their ineffectiveness by dismissing any other church that is large and flourishing as being superficial – we should be aware that Christ does not make surface analyses of churches based simply on their resources or the size of the Sunday congregations.

Faithfulness and success should not be set against each other, but we must concede that big is not necessarily beautiful.

> ### Press to reply
>
> **Is your church faithful? Successful? Both? Or neither? Why?**

5. Suffering, opposition and opportunity co-exist

The church at Philadelphia was told it had an "open door that no-one can shut." Most commentators see this as an encouragement that there was a ripe opportunity for them to proclaim the gospel: the city built as a mission outpost for Greek culture could become a mission centre for Christ. Paul used the term 'open door' to describe similar opportunities (1 Cor 16:8–9, Col 4:3, 2 Cor 2:2).

A PILLAR IN GOD'S TEMPLE

Christ gives a special pledge to the overcomer: "Him who overcomes I will make a pillar in the temple of my God. Never again will he leave it. I will write on him the name of my God and the name of the city of my God, the new Jerusalem, which is coming down out of heaven from my God; and I will also write on him my new name" (v12).

What could be more appropriate to the active evangelists in Philadelphia? The same promise applies to us. If we renounce in this life the way of ease, we shall in the next life, in God's temple which is heaven, be made pillars, stable, immovable, secure, which would not fall even if Samson were to lean on them. Philadelphian Christians might live in fear of earthquake shocks, but nothing will shake them when they stand as pillars in heaven.

If, then, we become a pilgrim in this life, we will be a pillar in the next. If we dare to go out through the door of service, we will never go out of the security of paradise. If we risk our name for Christ in this world, then on our pillar in the next, three names will be permanently engraved. The first will be the name of God, the second the name of the New Jerusalem (the church triumphant), and the third Christ's own new name, that is to say (since the name stands for the one named), we shall belong for ever to God, to Christ and to his people, and shall continually grow in our knowledge of them. That is the prospect for all who go forth valiantly through open doors, wage war against the powers of evil, and conquer in the fight. It is the promise of Christ; it is true.

– John Stott

A pillar from an early church in Philadelphia (modern day Alasehir).

Journeying with Jesus

You've got Mail

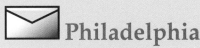

Jesus writes to his church

 Philadelphia

These are the words of him who is holy and true, who holds the key of David. What he opens no one can shut, and what he shuts no one can open. I know your deeds. See, I have placed before you an open door that no one can shut.

Rev 3:7

"It seems certain that the door which stood open before the Philadelphian church was the door of opportunity. Openings for the spread of the gospel were many and great in the Roman Empire of the first century AD. The Pax Romana permitted Christian evangelists to go about their business with comparative freedom, speaking the common Greek language, treading the fine Roman roads and using as their textbook the Septuagint (Greek) version of the Old Testament. In addition, wherever they went, they found groping minds and hungry hearts. The old pagan superstitions were being abandoned. The Holy Spirit was stirring the thoughts and desires of ordinary men and women. Many thirsty souls were panting for the water of life. Paul found this everywhere."

– John Stott

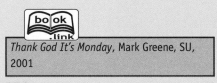

Thank God It's Monday, Mark Greene, SU, 2001

132

DON'T DELAY
Sometimes we can be guilty of waiting for more favourable circumstances before we get on with the hard work of being church and reaching out to our communities.

Philadelphia was small. Paul's open door sessions brought opposition. Opportunity does not mean an absence of difficulty. We can use a wide range of excuses to justify our unwillingness to be mission people:

- Our area is a hard area.
  Probably nowhere near as hard as Smyrna or Philadelphia.

- We just don't have the resources to spend on evangelism.
  Resources were very low, particularly in Smyrna.

- Our area is filled with middle- to upper-class people who are so affluent that they just don't see their need for God.
  Smyrna was one of the richest cities in Asia Minor.

- We have not been given a word from God to reach out.
  Matthew 28:19 seems quite clear.

- We're just praying that revival will come, and then everything will be easier.
  Smyrna and Philadelphia were staring at the very real threat of bloody persecution – anything but a revival receptivity to the gospel.

Behind you! Look at your open door

For the Philadelphians, the door was already open. They were just unaware of it, or had to be encouraged by Christ that he was the key holder of their opportunity.

OPEN YOUR EYES
Christians sometimes keep asking God for opportunities – and ignore what he already has given them!

Mark Greene sums this up as he exhorts Christians to see their workplaces as an open door.

- We are being called on to look for common ground with non-Christians, when, in the workplace, we already share it

- We are being exhorted to build bridges when, in the workplace, the bridges are already built and have been crossed

OPEN DOORS

▶ It is Christ who opens the door through which the church may go to share the good news, and we need to learn how to recognise an open door when it lies before us, and how to seize the opportunity that it presents. What might this involve?

▶ Be encouraged by the fact that Christ himself takes responsibility for opening the door. What he opens, no one can shut. It is his Spirit's work to create in people a hunger for God and to open their eyes to his truth. This will preserve us from frantic efforts to prise open doors which may be shut tight at the moment, and enable us to trust him to lead us to people who are responsive.

▶ Be like the church at Philadelphia! Don't wait until you are strong before being adventurous in mission, or you may wait forever. Count on Christ's power to use you more than on your own readiness to take on the world!

▶ Be ready to realise that there may be more doors open than you have previously dreamt possible. Since we know that Christ longs for all people to discover God's love through him, it would not be surprising if more people were ready to take the Christian message seriously than we ever dared to imagine. When I met someone who had become a Christian in his thirties he asked, almost angrily, 'Why did no one tell me this great news before?'

▶ Recognise that many people's apparent indifference to the church arises because they do not perceive that we have anything relevant or life-changing to share with them. There may be many reasons for this, but two in particular stand out. Perhaps they cannot see a deep and challenging quality of life lived out in the Christian community – either because it isn't there, or because we live it so privately that they have no opportunity to notice! Or perhaps the language we use to express our faith rings no bells with them. It doesn't seem to touch their own concerns. We seem to them to be operating in a mysterious private world of religion that doesn't touch everyday life. We don't scratch where people itch. Christ himself understands their concerns and their experience inside out, as the letter to Philadelphia shows. He knows what the city as well as the church has gone through, and he expresses his message in a way that is in tune with that. He is a model for us. We learn to understand people by listening rather than by talking.

▶ Give priority to friendships. Only when we are involved with people in genuine, caring friendship will we learn what their real concerns are. And most people who are won to Christ are won through the influence of a friend.

▶ Don't work from the assumption that people are uninterested, hostile or totally blind to the gospel. Even in a very secular society, huge numbers of people are interested in spiritual values. This may show itself in concern about the environment, or in exploration of the New Age movement. It may surface in the sense of wonder at the birth of a baby. Such signs may not be evidence of a lively relationship with God, but they are signs of a search going on. We should see them as searchings to be built on rather than as inadequate ideas to be put down.

▶ Don't assume that people who have no obvious sense of need will not be interested in the gospel. The gospel is not a psychological crutch for inadequate people, it is good news of God's loving purpose for people of all kinds. For ordinary, well-adjusted human beings the starting point may be the search for truth or the appropriateness of thankfulness to God for the good experiences of life. Yes, they do have need of forgiveness for wrongdoing and for being out of step with God, but they may not realise that until they have begun to be attracted by another aspect of the Christian message.

▶ Recognise your unique opportunities. No one else has your network of friends, your places of influence. Ho Chi Minh, father of Communist Vietnam, was at one time a dish-washer in the Carlton Hotel, Pall Mall. What if a Christian had been there alongside him?

▶ Don't waste too much time lamenting the doors that are closed, but make the most of the open doors. Readers of this book who visit the seven churches may be aware of the enormous obstacles to evangelism in Turkey today. But there are 1,500,000 Turkish 'guest-workers' in Western Europe. In these new surroundings many of them are able to hear the gospel in a new way, and the fact that some are exploited as cheap labour should move Christians to stand with them in the struggle for justice.

▶ Recognise that mission is the work of the church, not simply of individuals. The door is open to the church community, not simply to enthusiastic individuals.

▶ The insistent life of a Christian community has great power to persuade. And if we are to keep going, we all need the complementary gifts and the encouragement of each other.

▶ Recognise that Christ's mission, however fruitful it may be, will always meet with some resistance. Then is the time to remember again that the outcome is Christ's own responsibility, and to trust in him who says, 'I have placed before you an open door that no-one can shut.'

– Stephen Travis

- ✉ We are exhorted to go and develop relationships with people but, in the workplace, the relationships already exist
- ✉ We are encouraged to go out and fish in the pools and the puddles when we're sitting on a lake full of fish.

> **Press to reply**
>
> **What are your open doors? What do you plan to do about them?**

RSVP

Smyrna

A few years after Christ sent them mail, there were problems in Smyrna. Ignatius writes to Polycarp: "If you love good disciples, it is no credit to you; rather bring into subjection by your gentleness the troublesome."

But the church there laboured faithfully in the gospel. One of Polycarp's disciples was Irenaeus, who had been bought up in the church at Smyrna. As an elder in Smyrna, he filled in at a local church where the senior leader had died as a result of persecution. It is also very likely that the Smyrnian church was involved in church planting in Lyons, France, which in turn had a daughter church in the nearby city of Vienne. These church plants suffered severe persecution, and had notable martyrs of all ages, including the 90-year-old Pothinus (the leader there) and two 15-year-olds, Blandina and Ponticus. Irenaeus went into the situation to regroup the scattered Christians and restore the church. He was a scholar, and an evangelist.

Other churches were almost certainly planted from Smyrna – and there were other martyrs.

Today half the population of Smyrna is Christian; the city is one of the great centres of learning and piety of the Eastern Orthodox church.

Philadelphia

The conflict with the Jews continued into the second century, according to Ignatius. Several years after John's letter, Ignatius found them having a furious row about leadership and tried to prophesy into the

ARE WE LISTENING?

A Story ...

A few years ago, a city centre church took several weeks to study the letters to the seven churches of Revelation. In the middle of this serious Bible study someone posed a question:

"If Jesus were to write a letter to our church family, what would he say?"

The church took this on board and began to think and pray over the answer. Their senior leader asked people to write with their considered reflections and he ended up with a large postbag!

▶ Some who put pen to paper ended up writing very different letters from those they had planned.
▶ Some set out to write but found they couldn't finish.
▶ Everyone who took part found God released them to a deeper level of prayer about the church fellowship.
▶ All agreed it was a worthwhile exercise.

Having prayed through the large number of letters, their senior leader preached a sermon with the title "Is this what Jesus is saying to us today?" This set out some of the common threads that emerged from this exercise and set a course for the future. Many of the issues raised are part of that church's active vision today several years on.

A Suggestion ...

Is this an exercise that would be helpful for you as a church? Could it help to earth some of the things the Lord Jesus has been saying here at Spring Harvest? How could we go about this?

▶ Agree a period of time for prayer and reflection
▶ Write down the things you believe the Lord is showing you.
▶ Share the findings with each other.
▶ Look for the common threads
▶ Act on what you hear!

A Word of Caution ...

This is not a chance for you to ride your favourite hobbyhorse, to undermine those whom God has called to lead, or to encourage division in the church. Let the Lord Jesus speak into your own life first -- and act on what he says.

"He who has an ear, let him hear what the Spirit says to the churches."

Jesus writes to his church

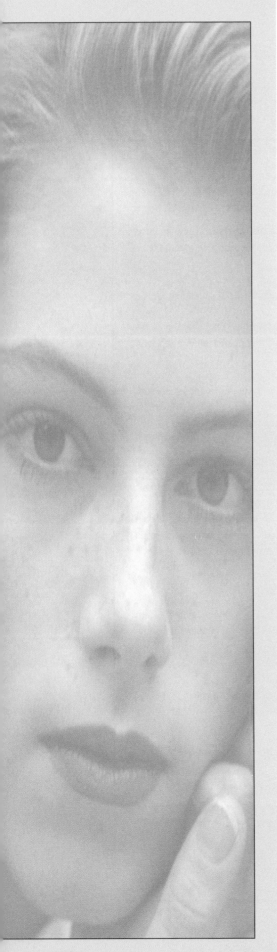

situation: "Give heed to the minister, and to the presbytery and to the deacons. Do nothing without the bishop. Keep your flesh as the temple of God. Love unity. Flee from divisions. Be imitators of Jesus, as he also was of his Father."

Some in the church wondered if he had been briefed about the situation before prophesying – which is not wholly negative. This response shows that they refused to treat prophecy with immaturity but wanted to be sure it was from God.

But the church struggled with division. Factions formed and there were separate communion services. And a leadership crisis developed, due to the weak leadership style of a quiet, gentle and unnamed man. It seems that the disputes were centred around personal rivalries rather than doctrine. And the church had to be rebuked for lack of hospitality to visitors – two of Ignatius' friends were treated with disrespect when they visited the church. The church at Philadelphia (which ironically means 'brotherly love') was lacking in that vital area. Ignatius called them all to gather around the centrality of Christ Jesus.

There was also good news and faithfulness ahead. The church had a highly charismatic lady leader later in second century. Ammia was a fine preacher and trusted prophetess. She enjoyed the full support of the leaders at Philadelphia, and apparently was an agent in the healing of division. Further persecution broke out, and there were Philadelphian martyrs – including Germanicus, a 'man of noble birth' who was terrified of physical suffering but refused to deny Christ. When faced with the crisis of martyrdom, he found the grace of God and actually encouraged the wild beasts to come after him. Others were tortured, and none yielded. Philadelphia birthed good teachers and eternal martyrs.

In later days, when Islam swept across Asia Minor, Philadelphia was one of the last bastions of Christianity. The Christians of Byzantium, who were jealous and desired its honour for themselves, ultimately betrayed it.

To this day Philadelphia is a Christian town with a Christian bishop. It is still a town of considerable size – now called Allahshehr, or 'the city of God.'

Teach us, Holy Father, to hope in your name.

You, from whom everything that exists has come into being.

Open our inward eyes to recognise you, even though
you are the highest in high heaven, the Holy One among
the ranks of all the holy.

You, Lord God, bring down the proud
and outwit the cunning.

You promote the humble and make the arrogant fall.

You hold in your hand every issue of life: whether we are to
be poor or rich, whether we are to live or to die.

You see every spirit, good or evil, and read the inmost
thoughts and intentions of every heart.

When we are in danger, you come to our aid.

When we are feeling desperate, you save
us from our sense of failure.

When events in the world overshadow us, help
us to remember who you are: the Creator and
Overseer of every living being.

– Clement of Rome, a contemporary of John the apostle
– adapted from After the Gospels, *David Winter*

MAIL FOR YOUR CHURCH

Designed for those in local church leadership, here are some questions to help you think through the implications of today's material for your congregation.

The Church Helps Those who Suffer

How does the church help those who suffer?

Think as broadly as possible about how people are helped by the church in the community when they suffer.

▶ What do the church's services and worship life offer those who need comfort and healing?

▶ Are these accessible for people who are not regular attenders?

▶ Are there ways in which the church exercises a healing ministry?

▶ How does the church share a prayer ministry that is open to all and encourages active participation? This could range from lighting candles to a prayer board, a prayer chain, an open church with said simple liturgy, or healing services.

The Extraordinary Situation

▶ How does the church react to national/international crises?

▶ How does this meet the needs or the response of the wider community?

Long-term Projects and Relationships in the Community

Ways for the church to care in the wider community.

Does the church have connections with or make provision for:

▶ the bereaved?

▶ the employed?

▶ the housebound?

▶ the retired?

▶ young families?

▶ marriage/relationships etc.?

▶ homes for the elderly?

▶ Samaritans?

▶ the disabled?

▶ the relief of poverty?

▶ other charities?

What persecution does the church bring upon itself by separatist theology?

What Does a Successful Church Look Like?

▶ How does Jesus identify success?

▶ How do we identify success?

▶ What realistic decisions could we make to become more successful?

▶ What are our goals over the next 2/5/10 years?

A LONG SUFFERING
COMMUNITY

MARRIAGE ZONE

Questions to apply today's material to marriage

1. How do pressure and suffering affect the marital relationship? What are your strategies for coping with stress?
2. Part of enabling a *longsuffering* attitude in marriage is the ability to forgive and deal with guilt. Are there areas in your marriage where you have retained the right to remind and accuse?
3. How have you dealt with crises of faith as a couple? Are you able to share your doubts and fears together?
4. Is yours a 'successful' marriage? How is true success to be measured?
5. Are their specific 'open doors' that God is giving you as a couple together? How are the different seasons of life (children leaving home, retirement, etc.) to be perceived as open doors?

Spring Harvest 2002
Church Leadership Stream

A Spring Harvest programme in partnership with CWR

PASTORAL CARE TODAY

Practise, problems and priorities in today's church

What a calling it is to serve God's people! Paul says to Timothy, "To aspire to leadership is an honourable ambition" (1 Tim 3:1 NEB). But it isn't easy. Caring for souls in today's fast moving and complex world is hard work. Leaders need the best support possible.

For nearly four decades, CWR has been providing training and resources for leaders. With a desire to provide as relevant resources as possible, CWR, in partnership with others, initiated the most comprehensive piece of research ever undertaken into perceptions and practice of pastoral care in the UK, publishing the findings as *Pastoral Care Today: Practice, Problems and Priorities in Today's Church*. When approached by Spring Harvest, CWR was pleased to partner with them on a project to develop the leadership stream for the 2002 event. It is hoped this programme will be a positive response to the findings and will inform, inspire and encourage as well as provide practical resources for leaders.

The programme blends material that provides a biblical foundation, statistical information, practical personal development workshops, the top four pastoral training needs declared by leaders, frameworks for pastoral ministry and sessions that connect leaders to the main theme of Spring Harvest. It is our sincere hope that the programme helps those in pursuit of such an "honourable ambition".

A positive response to the most comprehensive research ever undertaken among UK Church Leaders into pastoral ministry.

Journeying with Jesus

You've got MaiL

Jesus writes to his church

"To aspire to leadership is an honourable ambition "

– 1 Tim 3:1 (NEB)

"The pastoral ministry is probably the most difficult, but certainly the most glorious job on this planet."

– Rowland Croucher

Each session is "standalone"; however, it is strongly recommended that you attend the whole programme.

A POSITIVE RESPONSE

The programme has been specially designed to be a positive response to the research findings but also to carefully link with the main theme for Spring Harvest.

1. Biblical Foundation
Biblical exposition for leaders giving a fresh perspective on how Revelation is "the most pastoral book in the Bible"

2. Leadership Zone
Senior and experienced leaders bringing a leadership perspective on the main theme of Spring Harvest

3. Personal Development
Practical workshops looking at specific areas of personal development

4. Pastoral Issues
The top four pastoral issues that leaders identified as needing training to help others

5. Frameworks
A unique framework for understanding people, problems and how to grow health into your church

The morning Biblical Foundation sessions mirror, and complement, the Main Bible Readings by taking John's angle of vision as a leader and exploring his pastoral strategy as a leader in the church.

The four main morning sessions are …
John the Pastoral Theologian
   – helping the church see a bigger God
John the Pastoral Prophet
   – helping the church to be the church
John the Pastoral Exile
   – helping the church maintain cultural distinctiveness
John the Pastoral Visionary
   – helping the church to see ultimate issues

FACTS, FIGURES AND QUOTES

- 38% of leaders feel overwhelmed by pastoral demands
- 53% have felt like leaving the ministry
- When asked about physical, mental and spiritual health, leaders feel least positive about spiritual health. "Comparatively few pastors appear to be provided with the appropriate professional support to maintain the delivery of effective pastoral care. If leaders' wives provide the main source of pastoral care for leaders, how are churches equipping them to fulfil this role?"
- "These figures suggest that pastors may be seeking in-service training opportunities across a wide range of pastoral issues"
- "Pastors are relating their in-service training needs very closely to their perception of pastoral need most pressing in the world today"
- "These figures reveal a low level of contact between pastor and many key groups in the local community"
- "While the leaders place 'preaching' on the top of their own list, they feel that their congregations place 'pastor' at the top of the list of expectations"
- "Pastors feel that their congregations expect them to be administrators, managers and fundraisers, but they do not themselves relish these roles"
- "The pressures of pastoral life often make it very difficult to live out the life of prayer"
- 55% feel they have someone to whom they are accountable
- 50% set aside time for retreat
- 38% of churches have trained counsellors, 77% of leaders want to encourage biblical models of counselling, 14% encourage secular models of counselling
- "Why should ministerial training and in-service training be seen as of such marginal benefit compared With life experience?"

Published findings available from CWR, entitled *Pastoral Care Today*

– from the research findings written by Rev Professor Leslie Francis, The University of Wales, Bangor

Journeying with Jesus

YOU'VE got MaiL

Jesus writes to his church

Reversed Thunder: The Revelation of St. John and the Praying Imagination, Eugene Peterson, Harper & Row

The Theology of the Book of Revelation, Richard Bauckham, Cambridge University Press

A Practical Handbook for Ministry, Wayne Oats, Westminister/John Knox Press

Christ Empowered Living, Selwyn Hughes, Farnham: CWR

Stress, G Davis, Kingsway

The Hidden link Between Adrenaline and Stress, Dr Archibald Hart, Word

RESOURCE LINK
Living God's Way, one-day workshop available from CWR, 01252 784700

BIBLICAL FOUNDATION

John the Pastoral Theologian
Helping the church see a bigger God

This session looks at John's vision of God.

In doing this we remind ourselves that an essential feature of the pastoral task is to raise the sights of the church to a larger view of God's greatness and to re-establish the God-centredness of the church in focus and experience.

John as a theological pastor and lover of God is…

- in receipt of revelation from God, a recipient of God's word 1:1
- caught up in the drama of the God "who was, and who is, and is to come, …" 1:8
- enfolded by the grace of the trinitarian God 1:4–6
- directed to the praise and glory of God 1:6^b
- orientated with everything that exists to the throne of God 4:1ff
- focussed on worship as the supreme priority of the church 4:8ff
- convinced of the One Creator, God's intention to supplant the city of man with the city of God as symbol of his aim to renew all his entire creation 17–22

The overriding priority of leadership is to hear, receive and live out God's revelation, "the word of God and the testimony of Jesus."

Question

Is the lip service we give the Bible as authoritative and normative really put into effect in the way we lead and teach and disciple people?

Aim

To encourage pastoral leaders to give attention to letting God speak, to find their identity as servants of God not chaplains of the culture and to exemplify and promote God-centredness – in sharp contrast to the self-absorption of contemporary culture and much of contemporary Christianity.

CHURCH LEADERSHIP

REMARKABLE VISION

In John's visions we have a remarkable doxological framework.

"The theologian offers his or her mind in the service of saying 'God' in such a way that God is not reduced or packaged or banalised, but known and contemplated and adored, with the consequence that our lives are not cramped into what we can express but exalted by what we worship."

– *Subversive Spirituality, Eugene Peterson*

NO DREAM, IT'S A FACT

"Piously or politically, we cripple ourselves with the need to bring about God's righteousness on earth, failing to bear what Jesus so vividly declares: that we need not shoulder the burden because the goal itself does not need to be accomplished. The goal is a fact, God's fact, the fact of grace and promise. No gap divides what God says from what God does; and the stories of the coming kingdom do not offer dreams and possibilities of what the lord might or could do, but speak indicatively and in the present tense, of what is happening, and of what the future is becoming. The kingdom need not – and cannot – be worked for; it may only be accepted and awaited."

– *Between Cross and Resurrection; A Theology of Holy Saturday, Alan Lewis*

LEADERSHIP ZONE

Leading a Living Church

During the second session each day, the main theme of the event found in the various Zones will be discussed from a leadership perspective. See pages 8 to 40 of this Study Guide for notes on today's theme: Living Community.

PERSONAL DEVELOPMENT

The Leader's Spirituality

The leader's spirituality is a fundamental, yet often neglected area.

The *Pastoral Care Today* research reports 53% of leaders have felt like leaving the ministry. When asked about health, leaders feel least positive about their spiritual health.

How do leaders maintain their physical, mental and spiritual health in ministry? How do leaders take a rain check on their whole life? How do leaders live for the long haul and develop strategies to ensure whole person health in ministry, avoiding burnout?

PASTORAL ISSUES

Stress

In the *Pastoral Care Today* research, stress was seen as the most significant issue faced in pastoral care today. It was also seen as the number one priority in terms of perceived training need among leaders.

We all face differing degrees of pressure and people deal with it in different ways. There are two aspects to stress; an external pressure or pressures and our personal response to those pressures. A certain amount of pressure can be a good thing. However, for some, pressure passes a threshold and becomes stress. In today's fast moving world, a positive response to those experiencing stress is essential.

FRAMEWORKS FOR MINISTRY

Living God's Way
Introduction

Throughout time people have pondered the question of how problems arise in the personality and why it is that human beings are capable of so much good and yet so much bad. How do we explain such a dichotomy? Why do we behave the way we do?

Why we behave the way we do

Those who study human behaviour have come up with many different explanations as to why people act the way they do. The most reliable guide, however, as to what prompts human behaviour, is found in the Scriptures. There we find several significant keys that help us understand our deepest motivation more clearly than any secular theory. Through grasping these keys, leaders can help people live God's way.

The five areas of human functioning

1   **People are PHYSICAL beings**

"the LORD God formed the man from the dust of the ground and breathed into his nostrils… and the man became a living being." (Gen 2:7)

There is a direct connection between our bodies and our inner being. Malfunction in the physical can affect the functioning of a person's inner world.

First Key: Unsound physical functioning

2   **People are LONGING beings**

"I spread out my hands to you; my soul thirsts for you like a parched land." (Psa 143:6)

From the Fall until today, everyone has within them a deep desire that needs to be met. In their pursuit of happiness men look in a variety of places to have their longings met, but encounter personal problems when their deepest longings are unmet. "My people have committed two sins: They have forsaken me, the spring of living water, and have dug their own cisterns, broken cisterns that cannot hold water." (Jer 2:13–14)

Second Key: Unsatisfied deep longings

3   **People are THINKING beings**

"As a man thinks in his heart, so is he." (Prov 23:7, NKJV)

The first sin took place in the mind. Satan persuaded Eve to believe a lie, and once that lie was established it affected the way she felt towards God and ultimately the way she acted towards him. Since then, each one of us has deeply embedded in our thinking the foolish idea that life can be found by acting independently of God.

Third Key: Unnoticed wrong beliefs

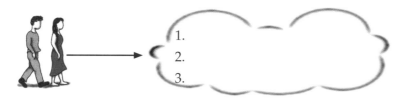

4   People are CHOOSING beings

"Many plans are in a man's mind but it is the lord's purpose for him that will stand." (Prov 19:21, Amplified Version)

Behind all behaviour is a plan. We behave in ways that bring us rewards. Many believe the only way to understand behaviour is to look back at the past (childhood events, perceptions, etc), but an equally valid way is to see behaviour as the result of choices we make, even though we may not feel we are choosing.

Fourth Key: Unrecognised wrong goals

5   People are FEELING beings

"It is right for me to feel this way about all of you, …" (Phil 1:7)

From time to time everyone experiences negative feelings – some of these can become extremely incapacitating and hinder our daily functioning. Negative emotions are, as someone put it, God's warning system to draw our attention to spiritual malfunction in our personality. These signal emotions always tell us something about our goals, the wrong beliefs fuelling the energy that directs those goals, and the state and condition of the deepest parts of our soul.

Fifth Key: Unsettling negative emotions

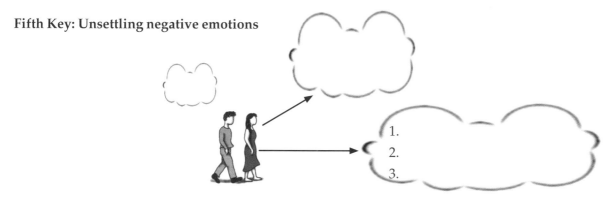

How do we keep people on track?

Whenever we find ourselves, or others, off track spiritually, we must takes steps to recover and maintain our close relationship with the Saviour. Having seen how each area of our personality has been affected by the Fall we now consider the steps we need to take if we are to overcome the damage to our souls.

Five steps to help people overcome damage to their souls:

1. Care for our physical wellbeing
2. Tune into our deep longings
3. Change our thinking
4. Understand the energy behind behaviour
5. Learn to manage our emotions

You've got Mail

journeying with Jesus

Jesus writes to his church

Revelation: 7 Messages Received, Selwyn Hughes, CWR

Leadership revised edition, Philip Greenslade, Farnham: CWR

Revelation: The NIV Application Commentary, Craig Keener, Zondervan

RESOURCE LINK
Marriage God's Way, Selwyn Hughes, Farnham: CWR

RESOURCE LINK
Myers Briggs Workshop and Team Dynamic Days, CWR 01252 784700

RESOURCE LINK
Research & Consultancy on Personality Theory Centre for Ministry Studies, University of Wales, Bangor, 01248 382768

Personality Type Scripture, Leslie Francis, London: Mowbray

BIBLICAL FOUNDATION

John the Prophet

Revelation 1:3–7, 22:7ff – This session looks at John's view of and vision for the church. We are reminded that the pastoral task is to help the church be the church for the world's sake and for God's sake. Following John, it does this, in particular, by re-establishing Jesus as the only cause and criterion of the church's existence. Echoes of this view of Jesus in 1:12–20 are heard at the beginning and end of each letter.

John the Pastoral Prophet
Helping the church be the church

John as prophetic pastor to the church (Rev 1:3) who "in the Spirit" (1:9–10) receives prophetic inspiration (cf. 22:18–19) and sees behind the scenes to God's victory in Jesus Christ.

This explains the book's urgency and relevance as a timely message for its day.

The letters are addressed to particular situations and introduce the whole series of visions and messages for the churches by offering:

- **Prophetic evaluation** 1:3 – blessing (and curse) 22:7. Revelation is not meant as a fix for our morbid speculative curiosity but as a prophetic message to be heard and obeyed
- **Prophetic encouragement** 1:5–6 answering the real questions and not the felt needs of God's people
- **Prophetic expectation** 1:7 for John, eschatology is applied pastoral theology offering a hope that stirs us to purify ourselves and maintain our courage, poise and sense of purpose
- **Prophetic exhortation** 1: 19–20, 2:1–3:28 to show that the church is measured by Jesus and is called to overcome.

The church succeeds not by gaining popularity or increasing numerically, but by remaining faithful to Jesus:

- a complete and innumerable company (7:4–12)
- whose prayers are 'bombs' (8:1–4)
- an overcoming church that loves Christ more than life (12)
- the remnant that paradoxically reverses remnant theology! (9:20, 11:13)

CHURCH LEADERSHIP

OUT OF LOVE

Revelation is a pastoral letter written to believers who needed to understand that God is embracing their present and personal history triumphantly.

– Paul Stevens

Revelation was not written for 'rapturists' fleeing from world, who tell the world 'goodbye' and want to go to heaven; it was meant for resistance fighters, struggling against the godless powers on this earth. It was written, that is, out of love for this world of God's.

– The Coming of God, Jurgen Moltmann

MIND YOUR CONTEXT

John's letters to the churches force us to attend to the context in the first-century Roman world in which his readers were situated and to which the whole of the book of Revelation was addressed

The book mirrors the situation of John's original readers during the reign of Emperor Domitian in around AD96.

Even more pervasive pressure for John's readers than external persecution was the insidious seductive pressure to conform to the idolatrous economic domination of the Roman Empire, sanctified by its religious system, which sought conformity and unswerving allegiance.

LEADERSHIP ZONE

Leading a Loving Church

During the second session each day, the main theme of the event found in the various Zones will be discussed from a leadership perspective. See pages 42 to 74 of this Study Guide for notes on today's theme: Loving Community.

PERSONAL DEVELOPMENT

The Leader's Personality

Personality is concerned with the science of individual differences. Taking people seriously, observing and understanding their individuality, stands at the very heart of a deeply Christian respect for the rich variety that God the creator built into the very essence of being human. Understanding the personality of a leader can play an important part in understanding the outworking of ministry.

The *Pastoral Care Today* research shows that different personality types perceive different pastoral needs in their communities, which affects the pastoral care strategies incorporated into church life.

PASTORAL ISSUES

Troubled Marriages

Nearly half of all marriages in the UK break down. All marriages have problems. The ones that succeed are those that face problems and deal with them constructively, strengthening and enriching the relationship. Many marriages start with love and commitment, but over time the amount of work put in wanes and less effort is made to keep it going. In the *Pastoral Care Today* research, marriage guidance was perceived as the second most significant pastoral need and the second highest-rated training need among leaders.

FRAMEWORKS FOR MINISTRY

Loving God's Way
Introduction
Jesus said all men will know his disciples by the love they have for each other.

We live in a self-centred society where people look after their own interest first. The world is full of hurting, uncared-for people. We in the church need to determine that we shall be a caring community, but this doesn't just happen. *Koinonia* fellowship needs to be fostered and nurtured. Throughout Scripture we see love. We see God's love shaping man, history and salvation. No wonder Jesus said:

"A new command I give you: Love one another. As I have loved you, so you must love one another. By this all men will know that you are my disciples, if you love one another." (John 13:34,35)

Empowering your church to care
1 Recognise the need for the church to demonstrate care
If you are going to empower people to care, empower people to present truth to others effectively, you need to recognise the need. If you don't see the need you will never seek to encourage and enable people to care.
1. The heritage of the church
2. Failing our responsibility
3. Restore our God-given role

2 Determine to make your church a caring community
The second key to empowering people is to determine to make our churches caring communities.
1. Caring doesn't happen naturally
2. We are too busy to care
3. The challenge is too great

3 Keep in focus that prevention is better than cure
The third key is the realisation that prevention is better than cure.

Level	Who	Outcome
Primary Care	Everyone	Health
Secondary Care	Life Issues	Restoration
Tertiary Care	Traumas	Reconstruction

4 Understand what it means to empower people to care
A fourth key – we need to understand what it means to empower people to care. We recognise the need, we commit ourselves to it if we say yes, we want a preventative programme – but what does it mean to equip people, to empower them to do it?
1. Gifting and development
2. Training and tooling
3. Doing and reporting

5 Recognise that effective equipping in caring takes time and commitment
Caring for people is a delicate and skilful process that requires great sensitivity and understanding. If we are not prepared to give time and commitment to equipping ourselves for the task, it demonstrates the low priority that we give to it.

1. Superficiality has failed
2. There are no short cuts
3. Requires involvement and investment

6 Select a core group who are willing and able to develop their skills
Everyone can care – it is part of the responsibility that we all have. It is not a specialised ministry, but it is helpful to recognise if we are developing a training programme that we need to take it in stages.

1. Everyone can care
2. Openness to growth and maturity
3. Start with 'people people'

The Christian church is uniquely designed to care
Several years ago it was discovered that there are three important ingredients for healthy human development – support, direction and a belief system. It was discovered that where there is not an environment that produces these elements, there is a strong level of immaturity. What better place outside the home is there for an environment of caring, loving community than the church?

Key Word	Function	Focus
Encouragement	Support	Feelings
Exhortation	Hope	Behaviour
Enlightenment	Transformation	Thinking

Levels of care

Encourage – a verbal or non verbal communication that supports people's feelings when they are facing or going through difficult circumstances.

Exhort – bringing a clear sense of hope concerning God's direction for life, resulting in character development and changed behaviour.

Enlighten – seeking to bring a new perspective and definite transformation from old thinking patterns to new thinking patterns.

book link
What Could I Say, Peter Hicks, Leicester: IVP

book link
Your Personal Encourager, Selwyn Hughes, Farnham: CWR

Your Personal
Encourager

Selwyn Hughes

RESOURCE LINK
Loving God's Way, one-day seminar available from CWR 01252 784700

RESOURCE LINK
Caring God's Way, Hughes & Partridge, CWR

Journeying with Jesus

YOU'VE get MAIL

Jesus writes to his church

Subversive Spirituality, Eugene Peterson, Eerdmans/Regent College Publishing

Imperial Cult and Commerce in John's Apocalypse, J Nelson Kraybill, Sheffield Academic Press

Honourably Wounded, Marjory Foyle, Monarch Books

RESOURCE LINK

Liberating the Leadership, Colin D Buckland, Distance learning course through London Bible College

A Practical Workbook for the Depressed Christian, Dr John Lockley, Word

BIBLICAL FOUNDATION

John the Fellow-Exile

Revelation 1:9–11 – This session examines John's attitude to the culture. It encourages the view that the pastoral is to restore the cultural distinctiveness of the church by helping it to face the tough reality of its cultural exile without succumbing to despair, self-righteousness or uncritical assimilation to the culture.

John the Pastoral Exile

Helping the church maintain cultural distinctiveness

John is an exilic pastor to the churches (1:9–10) training them in the discipline of being culturally distinctive through…

- being prepared to embrace suffering
- maintaining a kingdom perspective
- avoiding quick-fix solutions and building long-term patience
- being in the Spirit
- thorough-going commitment to Christ's lordship

A tale of two cities

Revelation envisages the clash of kingdoms (11:14ff, 13:1ff) and cultures as the tale of two cities (17–22).

The exiled Jews of the Old Testament were more than just geographically displaced. They had lost the structured, reliable world that had given them meaning and coherence. They found themselves in a context where the most serious, reflective Christians find themselves – increasingly at odds with the dominant values of consumer capitalism and its supportive military patriotism.

There is no easy or obvious way to hold together core faith claims and the social realities around us.

> "Reflective Christians are increasingly 'resident aliens'… I propose that pastors and parishioners together may usefully take account of this changed social reality of the marginalisation of faith…" (*Cadences of Home; Preaching among Exiles*, Walter Brueggemann)

Treasured and trusted symbols of faith were mocked, trivialised or dismissed. Exile is not primarily geographical but social, moral and cultural.

CHURCH LEADERSHIP

UNDERGROUND LITERATURE

"This is underground literature meant to create faithfulness to God and the Lamb in times of harassment, suffering and persecution.

"This is resistance literature that defies the Emperor and his propaganda machine, and unmasks the illusions of power and invincibility as the 'great lie'.

"This is subversive literature that refuses to say 'yes' to the Imperial cult and proclaims another as 'Lord' and 'Saviour'.

"This is martyr-producing literature that models bold and unflinching commitment to God and the Lamb, regardless of cost.

"This is revolutionary literature that creates counter communities of Christian resistance in the midst of the enemy's domain."

– Uneasy Neighbours, Walter Pilgrim

LIFE AS AN EXILE

Leaders must make people aware of their "exilic" location and train people to act and react accordingly.

This will raise huge questions of our preoccupation With evangelism and pressure for church growth and will make us concentrate our efforts on being more radically distinctive and refusing to be a consumerist option in the marketplace of spiritualities.

LEADERSHIP ZONE

Leading a Loyal Church

During the second session each day, the main theme of the event found in the various Zones will be discussed from a leadership perspective. See pages 76 to 106 of this Study Guide for notes on today's theme: Loyal Community.

PERSONAL DEVELOPMENT

Managing Yourself Through a Myriad of Priorities

Christian leadership can be very demanding, stressful and (reportedly) lonely. Leaders need to consider professional and personal development as a 'must' for a healthy working and personal life.

With many demands on them, how do leaders make decisions and choose priorities? This teaching session engages clearly with real-life issues that face Christian leaders today and will enable leaders to reflect positively, not only on their current working practices, but also on other ways of looking at managing self in the face of many and diverse calls upon their time.

PASTORAL ISSUES

Depression

Almost everyone gets depressed at some time or another. Triggered in a variety of ways, for some it is a matter of feeling down or low for a few days, but for others it can become a darkness and hopelessness lasting months or even years. While some realise they are depressed, others may not. They become lethargic and weary, or swing between periods of darkness and periods of unnatural elation and energy.

The causes of depression can be psychological or spiritual. Christians are not immune and in the *Pastoral Care Today* survey leaders rated it high in the list of pastoral issues they perceive and are personally involved with. Depression ranked third highest in the declared training needs.

FRAMEWORKS FOR MINISTRY

Prevent Small Problems Growing Big
Introduction

In this first part of the twenty-first century, the Christian church is going through what someone has described as a counselling explosion. This is in response to the fact that many believers seem to be struggling with enormous problems which hinder their spiritual effectiveness. While it is unrealistic to expect that every problem can be eliminated, what can we do as preachers and teachers to prevent small problems from becoming big ones?

1 A major problem in today's church

A common assumption in Christian circles is that psychopathology (the essential disease of the soul) is something that cannot be dealt with by normal activity of the church. The ministries of the Christian community – preaching, teaching and worship – have been reduced to a supplemental role in the process of bringing people to spiritual and psychological health.

2 Psychopathology – the real problems

It has been argued that the problems facing us in this century are quite different from the past and require a new understanding and a new approach. But is this really so? Is it possible that though there may be new and different symptoms the root causes remain the same? Human problems ought to be defined in a way that enables them to be dealt with through the pulpit as well as the counselling room.

3 Personal problems the pulpit can address

Christians hold different views on what underlies such things as anxiety, guilt and fear. If, however, we can understand the process of problem development then we shall be better able to address it from the pulpit. Consider first the most prevalent models for understanding people in the church today:

- The medical model
- The moral model
- The recovery model
- The spiritual model
- The deliverance model

In order to deal more effectively with human problems from the level of the pulpit or the teaching podium, it is essential that one has a clear and biblical view of how problems arise in the personality.

It has been suggested that the following five areas provide a simple yet helpful framework for understanding this:

1. People are physical beings
2. People are longing beings
3. People are thinking beings
4. People are choosing beings
5. People are feeling beings

4 Categories of mental health

Mental health professionals tend to describe the various stages of mental ill health as pre-neurotic, neurotic and psychotic. Consider how these stages can be explained in terms of a biblical model of the personality.

Pre-neurotic – when people feel resentful of their world, feel down on themselves or deeply anxious.

Neurotic – when people tire of trying to overcome obstacles and look for a safer existence away from painful feelings such as worthlessness.

Psychotic – the ultimate stage of withdrawal when people move into a world of complete unreality as a defence against the problems and pressures of living in the real world.

5 Teaching and preaching suggestions and principles

The more clearly believers understand how God means life to be lived, and the more clearly they follow God's design for living, the better they will be at handling life's circumstances.

First – search out and consider the many biblical passages that illustrate how prone we are to slaking our deep thirst and longings at a 'well' of our own making.

Second – identify the key principles that, when understood and practised, raise a strong barrier against neuroticism and psychoticism. Share these regularly with your people.

Third – illustrate through the use of carefully selected biographies the truth of how we can function effectively as people only when in a close and dependent relationship with God.

Fourth – realise above all that you can rarely take a person any further than you have gone yourself. Truth mediated through your own personality is extremely powerful.

book .link
Effective Biblical Counselling, Larry Crabb, Marshall Pickering

"77% of leaders want to encourage a biblical model of counselling."
– PCT research findings

book .link
The Christian Counsellor, Ed Richard Goodwin

Pastoral Leader On Line, www.cwr.org.uk/leadership

Journeying with Jesus

YOU'VE got MAiL

Jesus writes to his church

Cadences of Home; Preaching among Exiles, Walter Brueggemann, Westminster John Knox Press

A Passion for God's Story: Discovering Your Place in God's Strategic Plan, Philip Greenslade, Paternoster

The Hope of Glory: Honor Discourse and New Testament Interpretation, David de Silva, The Liturgical Press

Stress: The challenge to Christian Caring, G. Davies, Kingsway

Cover to Cover, God's Story, Philip Greenslade, CWR

Bereaved, I Knox, Kingsway

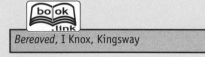
What to do After a Death, The DSS Helpful Booklet (D49)

BIBLICAL FOUNDATION

John the Visionary

Revelation 1:12f – This session probes the way John appeals to the imagination of his readers and hearers. The pastoral task is to reawaken the believing imagination of the church, to see into the heart of things as they are and to view them in the light of ultimate realities, so envisioning an alternative scenario to the one posed by the reigning socio-political system.

John the Pastoral Visionary
Helping the church see the ultimate issues

John is an apocalyptic pastor (E. Peterson). He is a visionary whose pastoral message comes in the form of an 'apocalypse' (1:1) and who communicates what he sees in an 'unveiling' that fires the imagination.

This explains the pictorial format in which the bulk of the book comes to us.

Key: the pattern is often what John 'hears' he then 'sees' and 'tells'.
1:12–18

> **John hears** a voice and turns to see Jesus glorified as the moral governor of the universe, in the midst of the churches.

4:4–11

> **John hears** an invitation to enter a doorway of perception and sees a throne.

5:1–4

> **John hears** of Jesus as the conquering Lamb and turns to see a suffering Lamb.

7:40–42

> **John hears** of 144,000 but when he looks he sees a multitude no man can number.

19:9–16

> **John hears** an angelic voice and turns to see the coming of Jesus.

21:1

> **John sees** a new heaven and new earth and a new Jerusalem.

"People are changed not by moral exhortation but by transformed imagination."

– Paul Ricoeur

CHURCH LEADERSHIP

THEO LINK

A GLIMPSE BEHIND THE SCENES

"John's work is a prophetic apocalypse in that it communicates a disclosure of a transcendent perspective. John (and thereby his readers with him) is taken up into heaven in order to see behind the world from the heavenly perspective. He is given a glimpse behind the scenes of history so that he can see what is really going on in the events of his time and place. He is also transported in vision into what the final outcome must be, in God's ultimate purpose for human history... . The bounds which Roman power and ideology set to the readers' world are broken open and that world is seen as open to the greater purpose of its transcendent Creator and Lord."

– *The Theology of the Book of Revelation*, Richard Bauckham

NO ESCAPE FROM CHANGE

The final outcome of judgement and salvation is told as the tale of two cities or a "clash of cultures" (Jerusalem and Babylon). But salvation is not to a privatised heaven but a renewed creation, not a going to heaven in escapism but a "heaven-coming here" transformation, leading to new heavens and new earth.

"Lacking an apocalyptic vision of newness, pastors can do no more than be therapeutic." – William Willimon

Our pastoral aim must be not to respond merely to felt needs, so as to adjust people better to the way things are, but to lead them to be reconciled to God's future in a new creation.

LEADERSHIP ZONE

Leading a Long Suffering Church

During the second session each day, the main theme of the event found in the various Zones will be discussed from a leadership perspective. See pages 108 to 139 of this Study Guide for notes on today's theme: Long Suffering Community.

PERSONAL DEVELOPMENT

Supporting Ministry

Christian leaders are not more important than other Christians but their role is crucial to the mission and purpose of the church. Healthy leaders can enable a church to be released to serve and enjoy the wonder of working in partnership with God.

Leaders report high levels of stress and pressure, leading to fatigue and ill health. This session is designed to inform and engage leaders in looking at ways in which they may experience support systems to help them maintain energy and health in their work, lives and relationships.

PASTORAL ISSUES

Bereavement

"Losing someone we love through death is perhaps the most shattering of all our experiences." (Rev Dr Peter Hicks) Occasionally death is something we welcome, a merciful end to long-term illness, the timely end of a long life, and in these circumstances the loss and the grieving might be less. However, at other times, if death comes suddenly or at a young age the pain of loss can be increased. Death is not the only form of bereavement. Divorce, retirement, amputation, loss of status and many other losses can result in similar sorrow and a grieving process.

In the *Pastoral Care Today* research, bereavement was identified as the third highest pastoral need and second highest pastoral issue with which leaders were involved. It is the fourth highest training need.

Jesus writes to his church

FRAMEWORKS FOR MINISTRY

Pastoral Care and Counselling in the Community
Introduction

Over the last decade there has been a process of continual change in the field of pastoral care and counselling and its impact on the community. Many agencies and churches have developed Christian counselling programmes and the growth of community-based Christian counselling centres has increased. Alongside these developments, the secular world of counselling and therapy has also developed, resulting in proposals to change legislation.

In all this change many leaders feel ill-equipped and some even threatened. This session seeks to provide a framework for understanding Christian counselling, pastoral care and community involvement.

The role of the pastor and the relationship to trained counsellors

The Association of Christian Counsellors, an accrediting body for professional and voluntary Christian counsellors, has seen a steady rise of membership wanting accreditation at the highest levels. Thirty-eight per cent of leaders report having accredited counsellors in their church congregations.

However, in recent research among accredited Christian counsellors
62% felt supported by their church leader
21% felt their minister perceived them as a threat
17% felt they were perceived as a complement to the ministry of their minister.

The "care to counselling" continuum

All churches desire to be caring communities. Some individuals are given special responsibility for care; others are engaged in pastoral counselling or outreach into the community, providing some sort of counselling service.

What are the risks? Where are the boundaries? How do church leaders develop training programmes for their congregations?

Christian counselling training and professional accreditation

What is the place of training in Christian counselling and of professional accreditation? Should church leaders pursue such training themselves or recommend it to others? What sort of training is necessary to achieve professional accreditation?

	Min Hours Training	Min Hours of Supervised Practice	Total
Level One	100	100	250
Level Two	250	350	600
Level Three	500	600	1100

Association of Christian Counsellors (UK)

CHURCH LEADERSHIP

Government legislation and legal aspects of pastoral care and engagement with your community

Ten years ago there was the possibility of the European Parliament establishing legislation that would have had an impact on counselling provided by churches or Christian counselling centres on the high street. This legislation never materialised; however, triggered by some recent high profile cases in the medical profession, the British government has plans to bring in regulation, probably in 2003–2005.

· What is the likely impact on churches?
· What is the likely impact on Christian counselling centres?
· What is the likely impact on the pastoral work carried out by churches in the community?

Setting up a church-based counselling programme

Many churches see counselling programmes as a form of outreach into the community. Other churches find hurting people attending with complex pastoral issues they feel ill equipped to care for.

· How does a church establish an effective pastoral care and counselling programme?
· How does a church provide best practical help?
· How do churches address the area of supervision?

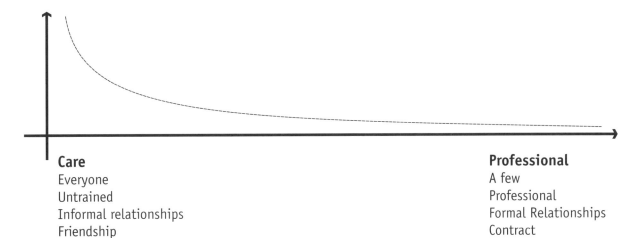

Care
Everyone
Untrained
Informal relationships
Friendship

Professional
A few
Professional
Formal Relationships
Contract

www.christiancounselling.com

Counselling in the Community, Altman

Through the Counselling Maze, Altman

RESOURCE LINK
15 Minute Life Changers, Selwyn Hughes, CWR (Eight titles available on request from 01252 784700)

Association of Christian Counsellors
www.acc-uk.org (02476) 449694

Journeying with Jesus

Jesus writes to his church

CRUSADE FOR WORLD REVIVAL
Applying God's Word to everyday life and relationships

CWR contact details

Waverley Abbey House
Waverley Lane, Farnham,
Surrey GU9 8EP
01252 784700
01252 784734
mail@cwr.org.uk
www.cwr.org.uk
www.christiancounselling.com

Acknowledgements
We would like to acknowledge the following people in the creation of the programme: The original research team, Sean Gubb, Rev Trevor J Partridge, Olaf Fogwill, Rev Professor Leslie Francis, Rev Dr William Kay and Mandy Robbins and those involved in the creation of the programme including Sean Gubb, Selwyn Hughes, Philip Greenslade and Colin Buckland.